H.C.
CHANG

Chinese Literature

VOLUME TWO

IN MEMORY OF
MY PARENTS

H.C.
CHANG

Chinese
Literature 2

Nature Poetry

COLUMBIA
UNIVERSITY
PRESS

NEW YORK
1977

Published in Great Britain in 1977 by Edinburgh University Press

Printed in Great Britain

Library of Congress Cataloging in Publication Data (Revised)
Chang, Hsin-chang, comp.
 Chinese literature.
 Includes bibliographical references.
 CONTENTS: [1] Popular fiction and drama.
—v. 2. Nature poetry.
Vol. 2 published by Columbia University Press, New York.
 1. Chinese literature—Translations into English.
 2. English literature—Translations from Chinese.
I. Title.
PL2658.E1C53   895.1′08   73-79265
ISBN 0-85224-240-9 (v. 1)
     0-231-04288-4 (v. 2)

Foreword

This book, a self-contained study and anthology of Chinese nature poetry, is the second volume of a projected series on various aspects of Chinese literature.

The series is addressed to the general reading public as well as students of Chinese. It does not offer an assortment of eloquent and moving passages from the whole range of Chinese literature; its aim is to give the Western reader a really close view of certain significant activities on the Chinese literary scene. Thus each volume will be confined to one or two types of writing, and will comprise fresh translations of works or portions of works chosen to illustrate one facet of literary history. A critical survey of its subject will be a feature of each volume.

The plan of the series is as follows:

○

Contents

○

Preface

The subject of this volume is Chinese poetry written in response to the world of nature. Under the title 'Nature Poetry' I have combined two traditional categories: 'landscape poetry' and 'rural poetry'. But I have thought in terms of poets rather than schools, and have presented a selection of the poetry of five important nature poets from the Eastern Tsin Dynasty to the T'ang, preceded by a survey of the feeling for nature which led up to its expression in poetry. For the most part I have allowed the material to define itself, having no preconceived notions on the subject.

I should like to thank my friends, Professor D. C. Twitchett and Dr D. L. McMullen, for reading my manuscript. As usual, I have depended on the resources of Cambridge University Library and wish to thank Dr M. I. Scott for valuable help.

I am indebted to Messrs Allen and Unwin for permission to quote from Arthur Waley, *The Book of Songs*.

H.C. CHANG
Wolfson College
Cambridge

○

General Introduction

The earliest Chinese myths recall a time when the natural forces were regarded with fear and suspicion by primitive man. They tell of ten suns that threatened to scorch the earth, of the firmament that was cracked by a giant, of a great flood that deluged the land, and of a blinding dust-storm that engulfed the Yellow Emperor and his righteous army. But, in the Book of Poetry, one already finds spontaneous delight in the countryside, in plants and trees, in hills, rivers and islands, in birds and beasts and fish. In particular, King Wen of Chou Dynasty, a model ruler, was accustomed to take his ease in the park built for him by his people:

> The king was in the Magic Park,
> Where doe and stag lay hid.
> Doe and stag at his coming leapt and bounded;
> The white herons gleamed so sleek.
> The king was by the Magic Pool,
> Where the fish sprang so lithe.
>
> (Waley, *The Book of Songs*, no. 244)

And the poem is quoted with approval by Mencius in conversation with King Hui of Liang, who had his own royal park:

> The king went and stood with him by a pond, and, looking round at the large geese and deer, said, 'Do wise and good princes also find pleasure in these things?'
>
> Mencius replied, 'Being wise and good, they have pleasure in these things. If they are not wise and good, though they have these things, they do not find pleasure . . .'
>
> (Legge, *The Works of Mencius*, i.i.ii.1−2)

In the Book of Chuang-tzu, xvii, also, we find the philosopher and his friend Hui-tzu standing on a bridge over the river Hao, engaged in a debate on Chuang-tzu's proposition that the fish in the water enjoy a state of bliss.

The mountain was an object of reverence from remote antiquity. In the earliest historical accounts, the Emperor held regular sacrifices at the five Holy Mountains, headed by T'ai-shan (in Shantung Province). Confucius, who had himself climbed the Eastern Hill and discovered the limited extent of the State of Lu, and subsequently T'ai-shan and realised that the world was but a small place, determined the Chinese attitude towards mountains in this pronouncement:

> The wise find pleasure in water; the virtuous find pleasure in hills. The wise are active; the virtuous are tranquil. The wise are joyful; the virtuous are long-lived.
>
> (Legge, *The Analects*, vi. 21)

Even as the virtuous take precedence over the wise in the Confucian scheme of values, so river and stream are subordinate to mountain and hill in all later estimation. A Han interpretation of the sage's words reads:

> The question is posed: Why do the virtuous delight in the mountains? The answer is: Mountains are what the people of the realm look up to with reverence. Plants and trees grow on them. A myriad things find a home on them. Birds flock to them; beasts rest on them. People from all directions obtain benefit from them. The clouds emerge from them; the winds blow over them. They stand upright between heaven and earth; they complete heaven and earth. They bring security to the State. For these reasons do the virtuous delight in the mountains. When the poem speaks of:
>
>> The lofty peak of T'ai-shan,
>>
>> To which all in Lu look up with reverence,
>
> what is meant is delight in the mountains.
>
> (*Han-shih wai-chuan*, Han Wei ts'ung-shu ed., c. 3, pp. 14b – 15a)

It was natural to associate longevity with mountains, which endure amidst all the changes that affect human life. In contrast, water is fluid and suggests motion; water flows and passes away:

> The Master, standing by a stream, said, 'It passes on just like this, not ceasing day or night.'
>
> (Legge, *The Analects*, ix. 16)

In any scene consisting of even one hill and one stream, solid stability is juxtaposed with liquid fleetingness. Thus contemplation of rivers and mountains underlines the contrast between transience and eternity, so that the mind hovers between intense happiness and despair, as described in the Book of Chuang-tzu, xxii:

> Woody hills and marshy lakes make me joyful and glad; but before the joy is ended, sadness comes and succeeds to it.
> Men's life between heaven and earth is like a white colt's passing a crevice, and suddenly disappearing.
>
> (Legge, *The Texts of Taoism*, The Writings of Kwang-zze, Part ii, xv, p. 73 (adapted); p. 65)

From the contemplation of rivers and mountains it was but a step to the taking shape of landscape views, and we may be certain that the royal parks in the Chou, like those in the Han, were laid out with some consideration of their pictorial effect. But it was several centuries after Ssu-ma Hsiang-ju's compositions in rhymed prose about Han Wu-ti's hunting parks that landscape came to be celebrated in poetry, for wild nature, as opposed to palace grounds or Holy Mountains, had to be invested with a definite significance. And it then required the pen of a poet with the eye of a painter to record it in verse.

With the breakdown of the Confucian order at the end of the Han, orthodox tradition lost its hold on scholars, and political confusion led to the dispersal and mass migration of the population. Men lived in constant peril all through the third, fourth, fifth and sixth centuries. There was a burning need for a new creed, one that offered transcendence of immediate and pressing problems, and immunity from imminent and lurking dangers. For Confucian learning and rectitude were unavailing against brute force, and Confucian etiquette floundered in the wilds of woodland or ravine, where scholars and their families, like humbler folk, sought shelter from the ravages of war. Selfishness and callousness had become the norm, and dissembled stupidity was a sign of wisdom. The physical environment loomed large in men's lives away from the haven of the ancestral village or the comfort and ease of a capital city. In desperation the teachings of Lao-tzu and

Chuang-tzu were seized upon for shreds of hope, and among the teachings was the doctrine that one should live in consonance with the principle that governs one's being, which is also the principle that animates all living creatures as well as the natural world.

The dictates of this doctrine set aside established social conventions, and people learned to lead the lives of individuals. There had always been a strong faith in culture, or the cultivation of man's innate faculties, of which learning was but a part. Freed from the greater part of their social obligations, they now turned their attention to self-cultivation; and in their self-expression they found a new ideal and impetus in identification with the cosmic principle. Among the arts, music and calligraphy were looked upon as the media that most approximated the rhythm and pulse of the universe. Wit flourished as never before or since. And the degree of personal accomplishment that marked many a man of eminence recorded in the Tsin dynastic history is quite astonishing.

Identification with the universe took other forms. Heightened sensation, suggestive of a higher existence and not unmixed with a sense of power, was sought by most. The habit of drug-taking to induce a temporary state of euphoria was widespread. To a lesser degree, fermented drink served the same end, and when the poet or artist or musician poured himself a drink, while not indifferent to its flavour and aroma, he was at the same time seeking a state of enhanced power and sensation, in which spontaneity could be joined with almost perfect control of medium and tool, in the form of words, or brush and ink, or musical instrument. Those with a Taoist tinge claimed, when in a state of exhilaration not necessarily induced by wine or drugs, to be in direct contact with the forces of nature and to be able to express their elation in a special type of whistling which evoked a response from the elements.

While the artistic imagination was quickened by intimations of a higher reality, those of a mundane cast of mind created for themselves a heaven in an earthly image. The goodness of the present life was never in doubt, and their essentially selfish outlook resulted in the desire to prolong their own full and happy existence radiant with talent and cultivation. With such an end in view, many took to living in the hills, styling themselves hermits and dabbling in alchemy, but suffering no hardships or privations, nor cutting themselves off from society except in (often a relatively short) distance. The quest for unlimited longevity proved futile, but none were ever disillusioned too soon, and the healthy air and the herbs and the regimen probably prolonged the lives of many, though not to the span sought.

To style oneself a hermit was indeed to have the best of both worlds, celestial and mundane. For honour accrued to the title of hermit, whose bearer was nevertheless at liberty to pursue his own interests and had only the obligation of finding a secluded place for domicile. And since gifted men often chose to be hermits, the prefects and governors and even the Emperor himself went out of their way to offer homage to, and seek the advice and instruction of, such unworldly souls. Now and then, a hermit of renown could be persuaded to reside temporarily at court or even to accept, understandably only for a 'brief' period, some actual office. But, whether sought out or not, the hermit had the company of the moon and the stars, the crane and the gibbon, the wind and the pine trees, which would note his spiritual progress.

The year 316 saw the collapse of the Tsin dynasty in the north, when the capital Ch'ang-an (i.e., modern Sian in Shensi Province) fell to the invading Hsiung-nu tribesmen. An exodus to the south began, and Nanking—then known as 'Chien-k'ang'—became the capital of the restored dynasty, the Eastern Tsin. Shattered by the fateful turn of events, the exiles from the north would forgather in some pavilion overlooking the Yangtze, seemingly their only bulwark against the invaders, to brood on the past and be pleasantly surprised by the beauty of the scenery. For northern eyes, accustomed to plains and plateaus and mountain ranges, the entire region that is now southern Kiangsu and the whole of Chekiang, abounding in lakes and hills, rivers and watercourses, was not short of a revelation. Chekiang, in particular, nursed the aesthetic sense for the apprehension of landscape. In the final years of the fourth century, the painter Ku K'ai-chih returned to his

post in Hupeh after a visit to Kuei-chi (i.e., Shaohsing in
Chekiang) and gave his colleagues this account of that
famous district:

> The landscape of Kuei-chi consists of a thousand rival preci-
> pices overhanging ten thousand ravines and gushing tor-
> rents, crowned by trees and luxuriant vegetation that
> appear like variously shaped coloured clouds.

(*Shih-shuo hsin-yü*, c. 2, Wen-hsüeh ku-chi ed., p. 95)

For the scholar-officials of the Eastern Tsin, the foreboding of
impending disaster added to the beauty of the scenery before
them. Indeed it was not until the redoubtable Hsieh Hsüan
beat back the invading Ti tribesmen in the battle of the Fei
river (in Anhwei Province) in 383, that men breathed freely
again. In the meantime, their own physical transference lent a
territorial significance to the words 'river and mountain', and
the dynasty's vicissitudes further accentuated the contrast
between human institutions, by their very nature subject to
decay, and the enduring universe. The lofty sentiments, at
once jubilant and mournful, expressed in the thirty-seven
poems written at the Lan-t'ing gathering[1] in 353 reflect the
state of mind, at once troubled and serene, of a select and
influential group. Among those present were the brothers
Hsieh An and Hsieh Wan, both Ministers at court; the
brothers Sun T'ung and Sun Ch'o, inveterate ramblers; Wang
Hsi-chih, a leading member of the powerful Wang clan known
to posterity as the supreme calligrapher, and a large number
of his family. The occasion was the customary ceremony of
purification performed on the third day of the third month, and
the place of meeting was Lan-t'ing ('Orchid Pavilion') in
Shan-yin in Kuei-chi prefecture.

To those poems Wang Hsi-chih (307–65) contributes a
preface that is a magnificent document in the history of the
Chinese sensibility. For it is the first considered statement on
the application of Chuang-tzu's doctrine of consonance with
the cosmic principle to the contemplation of hills and streams

---

[1] The poems may be found in *chüan* 5 of Ting Fu-pao (ed.), *Ch'üan
Han san-kuo Chin nan-pei-ch'ao shih*, Chung-hua 1959. In the ensuing
extracts, and for other fourth-, fifth- and sixth-century poems trans-
lated or mentioned in the rest of this 'General Introduction', the page
references are to that collection.

and, summarising as it does the outlook of several centuries, is a lasting part of the Chinese heritage. In the poems and in the preface itself, man's gaze is directed to the world he inhabits with childlike wonder. The eye does not rest on flower or tree or hill or brook as in earlier verse and in the Book of Poetry, but roves over them all in a sweeping survey. Not content with the delight this affords, the mind reaches out to the empyrean and beyond. What is more, man's cherished feelings not only find release but positively seek fulfilment in the natural world. The mountain heights, the sheer cliffs, the cascading waterfall, the echoing valley, the ever-widening horizon—these mirror the inner world: aspiration is assuaged by height; magnanimity comes into its own with spaciousness; solitude finds a ready harbour in the woods. Thus the Lant'ing poets will say:

I release my pent-up feelings among these hills and streams;
Serenely I abandon all restraints.
   (Wang Hui-chih, p. 438)
In these spacious surroundings my feelings find free scope.
   (Wang Yün-chih, p. 438)
Solitary aloofness seeks a home on this woody hill.
   (Hsieh An, p. 439)
I give rein to my feelings.
   (Wang Hsüan-chih, pp. 436–7)
In former days, when at leisure,
In my mind I roamed these woody hills.
Today I have indeed wandered hither;
My spirit is gladdened, my mind at rest.
   (Wang Su-chih, p. 437)
All my hopes and longings
Have as their limit these mountains and streams.
   (Sun T'ung, p. 441, under 'Sun Tsung')
I stretch my gaze as far as the lofty hills,
Then rest my eye on the woods near the summit.
   (Hsieh Wan, p. 440)
My spirit glides between heaven and earth.
   (Yü Yüeh, p. 443)

Preface to the Lan-t'ing Poems[1]
by Wang Hsi-chih

In the ninth year (353) of the Yung-ho reign, which was a *kuei-ch'ou* year, early in the final month of spring, we gathered at Lan-t'ing Pavilion in Shan-yin in Kuei-chi for the ceremony of purification. Young and old congregated, and there was a throng of men of distinction. Surrounding the pavilion were high hills with lofty peaks, luxuriant woods and tall bamboos. There was, moreover, a swirling, splashing stream, wonderfully clear, which curved round it like a ribbon, so that we seated ourselves along it in a drinking game, in which cups of wine were set afloat and drifted to those who sat downstream. The occasion was not heightened by the presence of musicians. Nevertheless, what with drinking and the composing of verses, we conversed in whole-hearted freedom, entering fully into one another's feelings. The day was fine, the air clear, and a gentle breeze regaled us, so that on looking up we responded to the vastness of the universe, and on bending down were struck by the manifold riches of the earth. And as our eyes wandered from object to object, so our hearts, too, rambled with them. Indeed, for the eye as well as the ear, it was pure delight! What perfect bliss!

For in men's association with one another in their journey through life, some draw upon their inner resources and find satisfaction in a closeted conversation with a friend, but others, led by their inclinations, abandon themselves without constraint to diverse interests and pursuits, oblivious of their physical existence. Their choice may be infinitely varied even as their temperament will range from the serene to the irascible. Yet, when absorbed by what they are engaged in, they are for the moment pleased with themselves and, in their self-satisfaction, forget that old age is at hand. But when eventually they tire of what had so engrossed them, their feelings will have altered with their circumstances; and, of a sudden, complacency gives way to

---

[1] *Ch'üan Chin wen*, c. 26, pp. 9^b–10^a, in Yen K'o-chün (ed.), *Ch'üan shang-ku san-tai Ch'in Han san-kuo liu-ch'ao wen*, 1887–93.

regret. What previously had gratified them is now a thing of the past, which itself is cause for lament. Besides, although the span of men's lives may be longer or shorter, all must end in death. And, as has been said by the ancients, birth and death are momentous events. What an agonising thought!

In reading the compositions of earlier men, I have tried to trace the causes of their melancholy, which too often are the same as those that affect myself. And I have then confronted the book with a deep sigh, without, however, being able to reconcile myself to it all. But this much I do know: it is idle to pretend that life and death are equal states, and foolish to claim that a youth cut off in his prime has led the protracted life of a centenarian. For men of a later age will look upon our time as we look upon earlier ages—a chastening reflection. And so I have listed those present on this occasion and transcribed their verses. Even when circumstances have changed and men inhabit a different world, it will still be the same causes that induce the mood of melancholy attendant on poetical composition. Perhaps some reader of the future will be moved by the sentiments expressed in this preface.

In the prefecture of Kuei-chi, where the cultivated made their home, men set the fashion of rambling among the hills. In the north, in the earlier reigns of the Tsin and before, the habit of wandering in the mountains was not unknown. One such rambler was Chi K'ang[1] (223–62), who, while picking medicinal herbs, often got lost in the mountains and was mistaken for a god by the woodcutters. But under the Eastern Tsin in the fourth century, what had previously been an indulgence on the part of a few eccentrics became a popular pastime. The brothers Sun T'ung and Sun Ch'o used their home in Kuei-chi to explore the surrounding hills, which they did most of their lives. Sun T'ung, who shunned office, asked to be made Magistrate of nearby Ningpo so as to be able to frequent the hills of that district. Sun Ch'o (320–77), now chiefly remembered for a rhymed prose composition on the

---

[1] See Chi K'ang, 'Letter to Shan T'ao' in Volume v of this series.

Tientai Mountains, was also one of the earlier poets who wrote on landscape.

The earliest attempts in verse at the description of landscape now extant were made by Yü Ch'an (286–339), who wrote about mountains and the hermit's life and whose two poems on the theme of the annual day of purification,[1] the third of the third month, pre-date the Lan-t'ing gathering by decades. One of the two poems is as follows:

On approaching a bend in the river on the third day of the third month[2]

For my annual dip in late spring I make for the clear waves
Of the stream, teeming with fish, along the ravine.
High on the hill to the east a waterfall descends
From a dried-up fountain now welling forth again.

As I approach a double bend in the river,
Where luxuriant woods blend with the lush, green grass,
My gliding boat submerges floating wine-cups
And my oar sends the fish leaping out of the water.

The description is based on personal observation rather than derived from earlier works, so that Yü Ch'an may be regarded as the real precursor of Hsieh Ling-yün. Sun Ch'o's poem 'Autumn Day',[3] which may more appropriately be entitled 'Day in Autumn in the Mountains', also contains descriptive lines, about thin woods through which the winds are blowing, mountain caves invaded by clouds and mists, the dew on the grass in the courtyard and in the woods, the falling leaves, toadstools, a pine tree. But the details do not hang together and there is no resulting scene or view, and the stylised diction conveys little original thought or observation. In so far as Sun Ch'o's mood colours his description, however, he anticipates Hsieh Ling-yün. Finally, Hsieh Hun (d. 412), leader of the Hsieh clan in Hsieh Ling-yün's youth, also wrote in verse about landscape views, although his descriptions mark no advance on Sun Ch'o's.

For the purpose of this discussion on nature poetry, the importance of T'ao Yüan-ming (365–427) and Hsieh Ling-yün (385–433) consists in this: they gave expression to

[1] p. 445.   [2] p. 445.   [3] p. 436.

feelings and attitudes in relation to the natural world cherished by others of their age who, being inarticulate, could not put them into words or shape them into verse. They mark the culmination of two centuries of development of the Chinese sensibility. In the description of landscape, as is clear from the brief survey above, Hsieh had little to model upon. And before T'ao, only the Book of Poetry provided glimpses of the rural world. Thus each unfolded fresh subject-matter, and each is credited with the founding of a new school—T'ao of rural poetry, Hsieh of landscape poetry. And indeed, as men, the two were utterly unlike: neither could have written even a line of the other's. It seems improbable that they ever met or knew each other's poetry, for T'ao began his seclusion at about the time Hsieh first became an army officer. And though T'ao was twenty years older, for the assessment of their achievements, they could be regarded as contemporaries. In the intensity of their response to a living cosmos, to whose pulse their own hearts beat, they were at one and equally representative of their age.

After T'ao and Hsieh had led the way, it was just a matter of acquiring skill and facility. Hsieh T'iao (464–99), known as the lesser Hsieh, was much influenced by his namesake, but his best lines are characterised by freshness of observation and directness of expression. In the highly artificial atmosphere of the southern court, interest in rugged grandeur and sublime beauty gave way to the pretty and decorative. Thus under the southern Chinese dynasties—Sung, Ch'i, Liang and Ch'en— few poets were chiefly concerned with landscape and the countryside, but most were skilled or facile enough to be able to include effective descriptive lines in poems on the seasons, on picnics and excursions, on friends setting out on journeys, on mountain huts and temples, and many wrote poems describing views seen during their travels or from some coign of vantage. Among those who wrote poems on landscape should be mentioned Ho Hsün (d. 518), Yin K'eng (died probably before 570), and Yü Hsin (513–81), who show a steadily increasing mastery of the line and the couplet and whose descriptions are often natural and lively.

That the eye and ear of many a literary man had been

schooled to appreciate sights and sounds in the natural world
is also proved by some letters of the fifth and sixth centuries.
One of these was by T'ao Hung-ching (452–536), who was a
pattern of the true hermit. T'ao, who was enormously gifted
and excelled in many branches of learning, was not too proud
to serve princes but genuinely preferred the solitary existence
of a recluse. The hill, Chü-ch'ü, where he made his home, was
not far from Nanking, and he was known as the 'Minister in
the Hills', having in a long life given counsel to the rulers of
more than one dynasty. When one of the Emperors sent a
message demanding what treasures or attractions detained
him in the hills and so kept him away from the court, T'ao
Hung-ching replied in verse:[1]

Your Majesty would know what treasures are hidden in
                                                    the hills:
An inexhaustible supply of white clouds floating near
                                                    the peaks,
A source of perennial delight to a mere humble subject,
Unfit to be sent as tribute to Your Imperial Majesty.

From a letter to Secretary Hsieh[2]
by T'ao Hung-ching

The beauty of hills and streams has been acknowledged
from ancient times. Here, high peaks rise above the clouds;
a rivulet, clear to its bottom, flows between rocky banks.
Before me is a pageant of colours with the dark pine woods
and the green bamboos flourishing in all seasons. As the
mists lift at dawn, the monkeys and the birds cry in loud
dissonance. And when the sun sets, the fish come out of
hiding to chase one another. This indeed is paradise on
earth. And yet since Hsieh Ling-yün, there has been no one
capable of entering wholeheartedly into the wonders of
man's natural surroundings.

Of two letters by Wu Chün (469–520), one gives an account
of a journey on the Fuchun river and the other of the scenery
in his native district near Anchi in Chekiang Province.

[1] p. 1234.
[2] Hsü Lien—Li Ching-kao (ed.), *Liu-ch'ao wen chieh chien-chu*, Chung-
hua 1962, c. 7, pp. 110–11.

From a letter to Sung Yüan-ssu[1]
by Wu Chün

There was not a whiff of smoke or mist, and the colour of the sky matched the hills. We drifted with the current, which bore us now in one direction, now in another. Thus we traversed the hundred odd *li* from Fuyang to Tunglu, through some of the best scenery in the world. The water was throughout a clear green, and over the deepest pools we fancied we saw to a depth of hundreds of feet; for we could see the fish swimming and the pebbles on the river-bed. At times the current was swift as an arrow and angry waves lashed our boat.

The hills on either bank were planted with coniferous trees and rose to a great height, seeming to vie with one another in steepness or eminence. There were hundreds of jutting peaks. The torrents dashed against the rocks as they came rushing down the hill-sides, humming and gurgling. The birds sang melodiously in chorus. The chirping of cicadas was interrupted now and then by the apes' shrill cries. Even as the eagle desists from its soaring flight when confronted with a massive mountain, so those engaged in governmental affairs would forgo their worldly ambitions if they set eyes on one of the mysterious ravines, shrouded in perpetual twilight by thick overhanging trees forming a screen through which the sun but seldom penetrates.

Letter to Ku Chang[2]
by Wu Chün

Last month I obtained sick leave and returned to the life of a recluse. To the west of Plum Stream is Stone Gate Hill, whose precipices reflect the afterglow of early evening and whose peak challenges the noonday sun. Clouds glide in and out of its hidden caves, and the gorge below it is verdant with luxuriant vegetation. The cicadas chirp and the cranes squawk; the torrents scream and the monkeys chatter. What a strange chorus of discordant voices, though with a tunefulness all its own!

[1] *Liu-ch'ao wen chieh chien-chu*, c. 7, pp. 114–15.   [2] *Ibid.*, pp. 115–16.

Having always preferred a life of solitude, I made my home there. It is my good fortune that the place abounds in chrysanthemums. There is also no lack of bamboo seeds, the staple diet and sole produce of those who dwell in this valley. There are no other riches, but it was not said in vain that the good and the wise find pleasure in mountains and streams.

A fourth letter was by Tsu Hung-hsün (d. early 550s) from Fan-yang (i.e., Chohsien in Hopeh Province), who lived in the north and served under the Hsien-pei dynasty of Eastern Wei and the semi-Chinese dynasty of Northern Ch'i.

From a letter to Yang Hsiu-chih[1]
by Tsu Hung-hsün

Being from a poor family with many ageing relatives, I have more than once had to leave my official post in order to be with them in our native district. To the west of the county town is Tiao-shan ('Eagle Hill'), a secluded spot with a clear stream and rugged rocks, surrounded on all sides by high precipices. There we have several hundred *mou* of cultivated fields. We had a villa, too; but the wars left it in ruins, and now I have had it rebuilt. The rocks provided us with a foundation, and the neighbouring woods supplied pillars and beams. The creeping vine adorns the exterior, and the stream winds round our front-door steps. The moonlight on the pine-trees and the winds rustling in the grass mark the boundary of our house. By the pond, like galaxies of stars, the yellow flowers of the leguminous 'Cloud Fruit' glisten under the dancing rays of the sun. The curling smoke rising from our hearth blends with the mists. Against the pines and firs in our garden, the peach and plum trees show up their green foliage.

Setting out from the house, sometimes I would lift my robe and wade through a torrent or with the aid of a stick walk up the peak. As I make my lone ascent, my mind becomes increasingly detached; my body would seem afloat and my very being ready to dissolve into nothingness. At such moments, I no longer seem aware that I exist on

[1] *Liu-ch'ao wen chieh chien-chu*, c. 7, pp. 123–5.

earth, and I would remain thus a long while before return-
ing home. At other times, I would sit by myself on a rock
overhanging the stream and play on my guitar to the sound
of rushing water; or recite verses in some concealed nook;
or raise my goblet and drink to the moon. The shrill
whistling of the wind would inspire my thoughts, and the
piercing cry of the crane touch my heart. Then I would long
for the state of untrammelled ease advocated by Chuang-
tzu, and approve of Shang-tzu's choice of the simple life.

At still other times, I would put on a coolie hat and a
rush-and-grass rain-cloak to attend to the sowing of the
millet and the planting of the rice, from which I would
return to wait upon my aged parents. My feet are now my
chariot, and I prize inactivity above all the useless bustle.
And I shall be content to live thus, forgoing even the
pleasure of good conversation.

Another writer of prose from Fan-yang in the north was Li
Tao-yüan (d. 527), the early geographer whose treatise 'A
Commentary on the Water Classic' contains terse descriptive
passages that are often striking and vivid. Later poets drew
on it for topographical information, and Liu Tsung-yüan, in
writing his landscape essays, profited from its example.

By the T'ang dynasty (618–906), the sentiments and
beliefs of the poets of the fourth and fifth centuries had become
part of the convention of poetry. Indeed they were part of the
stock-in-trade of every literary man. The response to nature
by the T'ang poets was genuine and spontaneous, but it was
no longer the passionate abandonment of the earlier writers.
Social and political conditions had altered, and men looked to
nature less for refuge and relief than for delight and solace.
The empire was again unified and at the height of prosperity;
communications had been restored and fewer places were unin-
habited. Moreover, landscape had come to be associated not
only with history, but also with earlier poets. Shan-yin in
Kuei-chi was Wang Hsi-chih's Shan-yin. Various areas of
Chekiang were Hsieh Ling-yün's haunts. Hsieh had visited
Poyang Lake, and T'ao Yüan-ming had lived in the shadow
of Lu-shan. To look at those places, or indeed any mountain
or river scene, northern or southern, was to see them through

the eyes of T'ao and Hsieh. Thus Wang Wei (701–61),
Meng Hao-jan (689–740), and other poets of their time
attempted with varying degrees of success the delicate task of
recording their own impressions and feelings about the
scenery around them in the diction of T'ao and Hsieh.

Szechuan with its diversified terrains, so different from
both north and south, proved a new source of wonder to the
T'ang poets. Mount Omei inspired the youthful Li Po
(701–62); and Tu Fu (712–70), late in life, described in
poem after poem the view from the towers and parapets of
Pai-ti-ch'eng (in Kweichow, i.e., Fengkieh) situated on the
heights overlooking the middle Yangtze gorge. But it was
left to Liu Tsung-yüan (773–819), a northerner born and
brought up in the capital Ch'ang-an, to discover afresh wild
nature, when for nearly ten years he lived in banishment in the
remote and sparsely inhabited prefecture of Yung-chou (i.e.,
Lingling in Hunan Province), a place devoid of history and
tradition but abounding in splendid landscape views. The
situation was not unlike that of Hsieh Ling-yün in his year in
Wenchow: the naked impact of the desolate scene on the
impressionable poet was unmitigated by local tradition or con-
genial society. Hsieh had been well read in *Li sao*, the work
of a poet in exile; and Liu was well read in both *Li sao* and
Hsieh's poems. Nevertheless, the experience was a novel one,
to be brooded over and absorbed without the guidance of
literary precedent. Liu had not previously been insensitive to
scenic beauty, but Yung-chou so sharpened his perception that
his prose sketches of the surrounding hills and ravines, pools
and hollows, and rivers and streams, make him the true suc-
cessor of Wang Hsi-chih, T'ao and Hsieh.

Of poets after the T'ang, two in particular are noteworthy:
Yang Wan-li (1127–1206) and Fan Ch'eng-ta (1126–93),
both of the Southern Sung. The landscape poetry of Yang,
who was from Kishui (in Kiangsi Province), often contains
effective descriptive lines, for example, 'On Entering Fowliang
County' (i.e., Kingtehchen in Kiangsi Province):

The moist sun is faint among the clouds;

The green hills are fresh after the rain.

The river half submerges the willows on the embankment;

The wheat reaches up to the shoulders of country lads.
Eddies suck in and spew the floating leaves;
The smoke from the stern is blown into the cabin.
A fair wind on a journey down-stream
Renders the happy-go-lucky traveller doubly lucky.[1]

Fan, who was from Soochow (in Kiangsu Province), wrote predominantly rural poetry, as, for example, in 'The Farmer's Year':

The plums are golden, the apricots ripe;
White spikelets of the wheat part yellow flowers of
the cabbage.

Not a soul crosses our fence the livelong day
Save only the spiralling dragonfly and the butterfly.

. . . .

In the slanting sun, thousands of cicadas chirp;
At night, a million frogs croak.
Fortunately I am deaf and in my dotage
Or I should lie sleepless on my bed of brambles.[2]

After the Sung, poetry lost much of its impetus, the energies of literary men having to some extent been diverted, in the Yüan and Ming, to drama and, in the Ch'ing, to the novel.[3] Interest in landscape also increasingly shifted to painting, Ni Tsan (1301–74) and T'ang Yin (1470–1523) being good examples of poets who were also landscape painters.[4] Few poets were associated chiefly with nature poetry, which tended to be derivative. A random sample from the Ch'ing is 'Chen-chou' (i.e., Icheng in Kiangsu Province), by Wang Shih-chen (1634–1711):

Along the north bank of the Yangtze fishermen dwell,
Where the willows show a gap by the lotus pond.

[1] From *Chiang-tung chi* in *Ch'eng-chai shih chi*, Ssu-pu pei-yao ed., c. 36, p. 3ᵃ. For Yang Wan-li's theory of poetry, see the chapter on him in Volume III of this series.
[2] *Fan Shih-hu chi*, Chung-hua 1962, c. 27, pp. 374 and 375; *Shih-hu chü-shih shih chi*, Ssu-pu ts'ung-k'an ed., c. 27, pp. 3ᵃ⁻ᵇ and 4ᵃ⁻ᵇ.
[3] See Volume I of this series; in particular Scene 8, 'Tour of the Villages', of *The Peony Pavilion* continues the agricultural tradition in poetry.
[4] For Ni Tsan and T'ang Yin, see the chapters on them in Volume IV of this series.

When the wind dies down and the sun is setting,

Under the reddening maple leaves they sell their sea-perch.[1]
In this book, I have confined my selection to the work of five
poets: T'ao Yüan-ming; Hsieh Ling-yün; Wang Wei; Meng
Hao-jan; Liu Tsung-yüan. Wang Wei's poems are accom-
panied by those of his friend P'ei Ti; and Liu's essays sup-
plement his poems. Each poet is represented by poems about a
particular locality that he knew intimately and to whose land-
scape he responded with feeling. In practice, this has meant
poems from a particular period in the lives of four: T'ao in the
years immediately before and after his retirement; Hsieh
during his fertile term of office in Wenchow; Wang in his
years at Chungnan Mountain and the 'Wang-ch'uan' estate;
Liu during his stay in Yung-chou: in each case, an important
period, in which the poet produced some of the best examples
of nature poetry in the Chinese tradition. With Meng Hao-
jan, who spent the greater part of his life in his native Hsiang-
yang, I have taken poems about that district without regard
to date or period. The resulting book, it is to be hoped, may
also supply the armchair traveller with an account of five
regions of striking scenery in China in the words of those
poets who first made them famous.

The principles I have adopted in translating the Chinese poems
in this volume are as follows:

1) On the whole, I have thought in terms of lines and
couplets rather than of words and phrases, the consideration
being that each pair of lines should complement each other as
in the original Chinese.

2) Each line is taken as a unit, within which as much as
possible of the meaning in the original is retained; but where
this would be difficult, I have not thought it amiss to resort to
paraphrase. I have tried to avoid literal renderings entailing
clumsy or awkward expressions in the belief that such ex-
pressions detract from rather than add to the meaning for the
reader.

[1] *Yü-yang shan-jen ching-hua-lu hsün-tsuan*, Ssu-pu pei-yao ed., c. 5b,
p. 11b.

3) The syntax is English throughout. I have not tried to reproduce the effect of the original Chinese by leaving out verbs and connectives that are necessary in English.

4) Within the line, I have regarded the word order as entirely flexible, as often retaining the word order in the original Chinese as changing it. In the second of a pair of lines, the word order usually either mirrors or contrasts with the word order in the first.

T'ao Yüan-ming

○

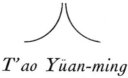

T'ao Yüan-ming

(365–427)

The story of T'ao Yüan-ming's life is easily told. He was a great-grandson of the famous general, T'ao K'an (259–334), created Duke of Changsha, although our poet's branch of the family was rather poor and not particularly influential. His name is variously given as Yüan-ming and Ch'ien, and it is conjectured that, with the ending of the Eastern Tsin dynasty in 420, he adopted the name Ch'ien ('Hiding') to indicate his final renunciation of the world. Certainly in his earlier writings he refers to himself as Yüan-ming.

His native place was Ch'ai-sang, the county town of which was some ten kilometres to the south-west of the prefectural town of Hsün-yang (modern Kiukiang in Kiangsi Province). The celebrated Lu-shan, which dominates the whole region, was but a dozen or so kilometres away; beyond the mountain was the vast Poyang Lake, then still known by its ancient name P'eng-li, dotted with countless islands. The area was indeed one of outstanding beauty, sought out by mountain-lovers then and since. Nearer Ch'ai-sang were small lakes, islands, hills, rivers, mounds and ravines. It was amidst such surroundings that T'ao spent his childhood in the country.

His father and grandfather had both held official posts. In a desultory fashion, T'ao himself also pursued the career of an official, serving in various capacities—civil and military—in the prefecture from about the age of twenty-eight, and making more than one trip down the Yangtze to the capital Chien-k'ang (modern Nanking). In the spring of 405, after such a trip as aide-de-camp to the local commander, T'ao resigned his commission. Already two years earlier he had thought of turning gentleman-farmer, as shown in the lines:

I have always known that tilling the soil is noble
But until now have not once borne a hand in it,

and generally in the two poems translated as 'Reflections on the farmer's life tinged with recollections of ancient recluses', in which he visualises himself in the role of farmer. There had been a small-holding in the family, but it would be erroneous to read these poems as an actual description of T'ao's life on the farm. When in 405 T'ao left the army, he looked at farming as a practical proposition and found that there was 'insufficient land to support my family of numerous young children'. He was now offered the position of Magistrate of P'eng-che, a county town on the south bank of the Yangtze about fifty kilometres from his home. (Modern P'eng-che, i.e., Pengtseh, is some considerable distance east of T'ao's P'eng-che.) It proved to be his last office.

Tradition has it that a routine visit by a prefectural inspector brought on a sudden feeling of revulsion that caused T'ao to throw up his post at the earliest opportunity, when his sister died at Wuchang (in Hupeh Province) in the winter of that year. The break with officialdom was now complete. The composition in rhymed prose 'Kuei ch'ü lai', here rendered into unrhymed verse under the title 'Homeward Bound', proclaims the beginning of a new life for our poet.

The rest of the story is to be found in the translated pieces, as told by T'ao himself. Superficially, the man shared certain attitudes with many others of that age—interest in natural surroundings, preference for the retired life, acceptance of poverty as the price to be paid for peace of mind. Behind the careless front and happy-go-lucky manner was, however, an incisive intellect harbouring thoughts of real profundity. Most significant of all was his trust in his own instinct, which from the start led him to a complete sense of affinity with nature, of which—for him—man was but a part. In an almost valedictory letter to his sons, written when he was over fifty, he says:

As a lad I learnt to play the guitar along with my studies, and came to love peace and quiet. And whenever I discovered something new in my reading, I would be overjoyed and would forget to eat. But the sight of the trees with their outstretched leafy branches and the sound of the birds'

songs which varied with the seasons gladdened me no less.
And I maintained that to recline by a north-facing window
in the sultry heat of the fifth and sixth months and enjoy the
cool breezes was a state of bliss equal to the boundless
tranquillity enjoyed by the Sage Emperors.[1]

This passage is a key to the understanding of T'ao. The
instincts of a village boy remained with him throughout the
bustle of affairs, the struggles to keep up the appearance of
gentility, the study and meditation, and the crystallisation of
experience in verse. The changing seasons, the singing of the
birds, the leafy trees, the fields, valleys and meadows en-
lightened him on the purpose and destiny of man. Of the pre-
vailing doctrine of consonance with the cosmic principle he
felt no need, for he was at home in the world of nature and did
not look upon it as something external. The breathless beauty
and ecstatic vision which others sought in natural surroundings
had no appeal for him, who found cause for rejoicing in a
single hillock, a shallow torrent or a lone pine.

The fanciful self-portrait done in his youth, 'Master of the
Five Willows', though interesting, reveals less of the man:

It is not known for certain where the subject of this bio-
graphy hailed from, nor what his surname and other names
were. Five willows grew by his house, for which reason he
styled himself Master of the Five Willows. He loved peace
and quiet, being a man of few words, not attracted by glory
or gain. He was much given to reading, without troubling
always to unravel the intricacies of the text. But when
struck by something in his reading, he would be so inspired
as to forget to eat. He was fond of drinking but, being poor,
could not often procure wine for himself. Friends and
relatives who knew about this would invite him to drink
with them. When he came, he would drink up all that was
laid before him, bent on getting intoxicated. And when he
was intoxicated, he at once took his leave without showing
the least sign of wishing to remain. The walls in his house
were quite bare and provided inadequate shelter from the
wind and the sun. Dressed in short, coarse garments, torn
and patched in places, he would endure hunger for days on

[1] p. 372; Ssu-pu pei-yao ed., c. 7, p. 2[a].

end with equanimity. To amuse himself, he wrote essays in which he showed something of his aspirations, and this made him indifferent to his worldly fortunes. And in this manner he ended his days.

In fine, the words that were once said:
'Neither grieving and sorrowing in poverty
or lowliness

Nor in hot pursuit of riches and fame'
indeed apply to someone like the Master of the Five Willows, who, with his cup raised to his lip, composed verses to cheer up his own spirit. Here was one surviving from the primeval days of the blessed reigns of the Sage Emperors.[1]

There are many parallels between 'Homeward Bound' and the five poems under the title 'Rural Living' ('Kuei yüan t'ien chü') written in the following year (406), and the two pieces are best read together. In the original, both titles contain the word 'kuei' ('to return'), and I am convinced that T'ao was returning to the native village of his childhood. Sowing beans under the Southern Mountain (i.e., Lu-shan) in 'Rural Living', III, has its literary precedent in a Han song, in which the singer retires to a 'southern mountain', where the soil is too poor to grow anything but beans.

The poem that forms a companion to Magistrate Liu's is to be read, as companion pieces should be, as an echo of the original. Liu's poem is not preserved, and the 'fair daughter' in line 13 ('One fair daughter, who—more's the pity—is no son' is how the line should run) has exercised the ingenuity of commentators, who have gone so far as to suggest that the phrase means a feminine or weak drink offered by T'ao's host in lieu of a masculine or potent spirit. Clearly, Liu's daughter is meant; T'ao himself had five sons. In his final years Liu was prominent in the activities of the Buddhist White Lotus Society on Lu-shan, with which T'ao also came into contact. The poem is, however, dated by the lines:

My ⎡i.e., Liu's⎤ thatched cottage is almost completed;
The reclaimed land soon enters its third year.

Liu retired to Lu-shan in 403–4; the poem must have been

<hr>

[1] pp. 364–5; Ssu-pu pei-yao ed., c. 6, pp. 7ᵇ–8ᵃ.

written in 405–6, at or near the time of T'ao's own retirement.

In 'An Excursion to Slanting Stream' we find the poet meditating on the scenery confronting him when he and a few friends visited that little-known stream with the island Wall Mount in the distance. The mood is a sombre one: river and hillock provide the setting for an almost solemn gathering; the poet is not only Master of the Ceremonies but also leader and spokesman of the small group. The result is a poem dealing with the larger issues of time and the moment, man and the physical world. The thought behind it is no more than the transience of life in an ever-changing universe, but, in its quiet and restrained manner, it is probably the best statement in verse of the ideas expressed by Wang Hsi-chih in the Lan-t'ing Preface. We also learn from the prefatory note about T'ao's reluctance to commemorate famous places.

In 'The Alternation of the Seasons' (probably written in 404, as has been suggested[1]) T'ao paints an idyllic portrait of himself at rest in his garden and hut after a walk in spring through the genial hill and river scenery he revels in. The prefatory note speaks of 'joy and pensive sadness' intermingling; commentators have pointed out that the first two stanzas are concerned with joy, the third and fourth stanzas with pensive sadness.

The original title of 'South Village' is 'I chü' ('Moving House'). It is usually dated 410; but 408–9 seems more likely, since in the autumn of 410 our poet was already reaping an early harvest.[2] After the outbreak of a fire in the summer of 408, T'ao and his family lived for some time on a boat moored before their burnt-down house. There was thus every inducement to move to South Village, whose congenial inhabitants included scholars living in retirement with whom he could discuss literary subjects. The second poem shows a workaday attitude to farming, reflected also in the harvest poems of 410[2] and 416,[3] not included here.

---

[1] See Wang Yao (ed.), *T'ao Yüan-ming chi*, Tso-chia 1956, p. 31.
[2] See 'Reaping an early rice harvest in the western fields in the ninth month of *keng-hsü* year (410)', p. 145; Ssu-pu pei-yao ed., c. 3, p. 14[a].
[3] p. 148; Ssu-pu pei-yao ed., c. 3, pp. 14[b]–15[a].

The recurrent themes of T'ao's poetry are the simple dignity of man, shorn of cultural adornments and freed from the restraints of society, and unqualified trust in instinct and in providence. Artificiality and shrewd calculation were alien to him. Whereas others of his age endeavoured and professed to live in accordance with nature, T'ao's mode of living was naturalness itself, as he states in the prefatory note to 'Homeward Bound':

My disposition was so inclined to the carefree state, it would not comply with the rigorous demands of artificial routine;

and also in 'Rural Living', 1:

One who has felt himself imprisoned in a cage
Returns once again to a life of careless freedom.

Thus the simplicity and naturalness of T'ao's diction are a perfect dress for the man's feelings. Even in poems in which the thought is subtle and complex—for example, 'Substance, Shadow and Spirit',[1] the language remains simple, consisting for the most part of plain statements devoid of embellishments. This simple and plain style of T'ao's, although out of fashion with the poets of the immediately succeeding ages, who preferred rhetoric to direct utterance and rated prosodic skill higher than innate rhythm, provided a salutary example for all later Chinese poets.[2] As regards rural themes and sentiments, T'ao influence on later poetry was pervasive and insidious. It may easily be traced in the poems of Wang Wei in the chapter on him, and in many poems by Meng Hao-jan and Liu Tsung-yüan, which it has not been found possible to include in their respective chapters in this book.

For my translations I have used the text in *T'ao Yüan-ming chüan*, Volume II, of the Ku-tien wen-hsüeh yen-chiu tzu-liao hui-pien series, and references in the footnotes are to that edition. I have also inserted references to the Ssu-pu pei-yao edition of T'ao Shu's *Ching-chieh hsien-sheng chi*.

---

[1] pp. 32–3; Ssu-pu pei-yao ed., c. 2, pp. 1ᵃ–2ᵇ.
[2] For appraisal of T'ao's poetry by a sixth-century and a thirteenth-century critic see Chung Yung, 'The Grading of Five Poets' and Yen Yü, 'Memorable Lines in T'ao and Hsieh' in Volume III of this series.

Homeward Bound[1]
(405)

Being poor, with insufficient land to support my family of numerous young children and no reserve of grain in store, I saw no means of gaining a livelihood. Relatives and friends encouraged me to take a post under a magistrate, and of this scheme I cherished some vain hopes. It was a time of turmoil and the regional commanders relied on personal patronage for loyal support, and my uncle, taking pity on my circumstances, obtained for me an actual magistracy over a small district. The realm not being at peace, I was reluctant to seek employment in a distant place; but P'eng-che was no more than a hundred *li* from my home. The holder of the office enjoyed, moreover, the privilege of the sole use of a measure of land, which I thought would yield a large quantity of millet for my brewing. I, therefore, accepted the appointment with alacrity.

But a short while after, I began to pine for home and to have thoughts of returning to my native village. What had brought this about? My disposition was so inclined to the carefree state, it would not comply with the rigorous demands of artificial routine. Though hunger and cold might indeed be pressing, I now suffered from the additional malady of fighting against my own nature. When engaged in the service of others, I but enslaved myself in order to appease my belly. With a rueful sigh I concluded that I had been false to my true aims. I looked forward, however, to the harvest, when I could gracefully retire after a full year's service. Then my sister died at Wuchang, and since I had to hurry to the funeral, I resigned forthwith from the magistracy. From mid autumn to winter, I was in office for eighty-odd days. In setting forth the events, I have but followed my own inclinations, for which reason I entitle the piece 'Homeward Bound', which was written in the eleventh month of *i-ssu* year (405).

Homeward bound I am at last!
The fields and orchards are overgrown with weeds — why
did I tarry?

[1] pp. 326–7; Ssu-pu pei-yao ed., c. 5, pp. 6ᵃ–8ᵇ.

I who have enlisted my soul in the service of my body
Am the sole cause of my regrets and unshared grief:
The past is irretrievable, now that I realise my folly,
But the future still is mine!
Nor is it far that I have strayed
When I know myself now to be right, though wrong
                                        only yesterday.
The boat rocks gently as it moves upstream
Against a wind which lifts my cloak and swells my sleeves.
I ask the way of a man on the shore
And under the faint light of dawn bend my steps towards home.

Once again I see the house and doorway
With joy in my heart and wings on my feet.
The servants come forward to greet me,
And my young son stands waiting demurely at the gate.
Grass has overspread the paths
But the pines and chrysanthemums are still there.
Leading my boy by the hand, I enter the house
And find that luxury—a jar of wine—on the table.

I pour myself a cup of good cheer;
I am gladdened by the sight of each tree in the courtyard;
At the south window the view defines my aspirations;
These rooms, though tiny, offer more than mere comfort.
My garden grows more interesting with each day's visit;
My gate seldom creaks to welcome a visitor.
Supported by a bamboo staff, I would pause in my ramblings
And time and again lift my head to gaze afar
At some mysterious cloud hovering near the mountain peak
Or the birds, weary of wandering, returning to their nests.
In the fading twilight before darkness descends,
I would touch and linger by a lone pine tree.

Homeward bound I was, and at home I am!
And I ask, too, to break off all ties with the world!
For the world's way is not my way,
And I will not seek the right of admission to it again.
I delight in the homely sentiments of near ones and dear ones
And beguile the time with my books and my guitar.

The farmers tell me with glee that spring is at hand
And they will start the year's toil in the western fields.
I would mount my chariot
Or set off in a canoe
To ferret out the secrets of some dark ravine
Or try the slope of some hillock.
The trees are running with sap,
The fountains are again trickling:
The myriad objects in the pageant of the seasons
Govern my alternate phases of action and of rest.

Alas, how much longer shall this my body inhabit the earth?
Why not be guided by my soul though I may too soon perish?
What was it I sought so busily and so restlessly?
Not wealth, not rank—these are not among my wishes,
And the sphere of the immortals is beyond my reach.
To walk alone with a sense of uplift on a fine morning
Or potter about in the fields, is all I desire,
To ascend the eastern eminence and whistle to the
                                                    cosmic forces
Or compose verses to the sound of a rushing stream,
And so end my days in accordance with the cycle of growth
                                                    and decay,
Rejoicing in heaven's will without doubt or suspicion.

Rural Living[1]
(406)

I

As a lad I was ill attuned to the loud, vulgar world,
My disposition being prepossessed by the still, silent hills.
Caught unawares in the net of pomps and vanities,
After thirty long years[2] I have set myself free.

---

[1] pp. 47–8; Ssu-pu pei-yao ed., c. 2, pp. 4ª–5ᵇ.
[2] The reading 'thirty years'—as opposed to 'thirteen years', which some editors propose—is supported by ll. 13–14 of IV:
    'The face of the world may change in a generation'—
    The proverb is here proved true:
the usual definition of a generation being thirty years.

The migrant bird seeks out the woods that were its shelter;
The fish in the pond remember thriving in deeper waters.
To my farm on the edge of the southern wastes,
I, creature of instinct not reason, have returned.

The field is but a dozen or so *mou* adjoining
A courtyard of eight or nine rooms under thatched roofs;
Elms and willows extend the eaves at the back;
In front, peach and plum trees provide a screen.

Under a hazy sun a village lies snugly yonder,
From whose hearths the curling smoke is rising;
Hidden in some winding lane, a dog is barking,
While from the top of a mulberry tree a cock crows.

Clean dirt only, no worldly dust, soils the house and courtyard;
The rooms, being bare, contain ample leisure:
One who has felt himself imprisoned in a cage
Returns once again to a state of careless freedom.

II

In these wild tracts I have few dealings with men;
Seldom would a carriage enter this lowly lane.
In broad daylight I firmly shut my gate
And debar all worldly thoughts from these bare rooms.

Now and then, to be sure, in some corner of the waste land,
Brushing through the long grass, my neighbours and
                                        I would meet:
When we do meet, the limit of our conversation
Is how the hemp and the mulberry trees are growing.

The mulberry trees and the hemp have indeed grown;
My farm, too, has much increased in extent.
But alas, the frost or the hailstorm may descend
And blast grass and hemp and mulberry leaf alike!

III

In a waste patch under the Southern Mountain
                                        I sowed some beans,
But the grass grows thick and the bean stalks are
                                        scattered and thin.

Early in the morning I set about the task of weeding;
By moonlight I return with my hoe on my shoulder.

The path is walled in by straggling plants and trees,
The evening dew on which soaks through my clothes.
That my clothes are soaked is no great pity
As long as my inmost self remains untainted.

IV

Having long been away from these lakes and hills—
Being glad again to roam the fields and woods—
I take my sons and nephews on a walk
Through the thickets and across the wastes.

As we linger among some grave mounds,
I see clear traces of former habitations,
Here an abandoned stone well, there a brick stove,
Amidst mulberries and bamboos, mostly withered.

I ask a man gathering fire-wood,
'Where have the dwellers gone?'
The woodcutter says in reply:
'All are dead, none remain.'

'The face of the world may change in a generation'—
The proverb is here proved true:
The life of man is a bubble
Ending at last in nothingness.

V

Feeling dispirited on returning from my lone ramblings
Across a steep hill-side and a glen overgrown with thorns,
I am cheered by a torrent at once transparent
And shallow enough in which to bathe my feet.

Having strained our home-made new wine,
I invite the neighbours to dine on a pullet.
When, after sunset, the room suddenly darkens,
The thornstick in the hearth lends radiance to our gathering.

Thus, our simple convivial pleasures so shorten the night,
Before we even know it, the day has dawned.

*A Companion Piece echoing the sentiments in
the Original Poem by Former Magistrate Liu of Ch'ai-sang*[1]

The hills and lakes had long beckoned to me —
Why then had I shown such hesitation?
For the sake of old friends and relations,
I could not bear to seek a hermit's existence!

And now, when in the mood I seize my moment;
I carry a stick and walk to my former dwelling,
Meeting along the deserted road no inhabitants —
Instead I am greeted by abandoned relics.

My thatched cottage is almost completed;
The reclaimed land soon enters its third year.
When the east wind brings on a fit of melancholy,
The season's new wine relieves thirst and fatigue.

One fair daughter, a priceless jewel,
Comforts me in lieu of son and heir.
Alarmed by the trend of events in the world,
We pass our time, heedless of its chronology.

We farm and weave to supply our own needs,
Beyond which is more than concerns us.
Thus cheerfully I shall end my days
Shrouding my life and my name in obscurity.

*Reflections on the farmer's life tinged with recollections of
ancient recluses, written early in* keui-mao *year*[2]
(403)

I

I have always known that tilling the soil is noble
But until now have not once borne a hand in it;
Since the scholar ever has been poor and starving,
How could I alone shirk the toils of the spring sowing?

---

[1] p. 88; Ssu-pu pei-yao ed., c. 2, pp. 12ᵇ–13ᵃ. Liu Ch'eng-chih, for
some time Magistrate of T'ao's native Ch'ai-sang, became a recluse
at Lu-shan from about 403–4.
[2] p. 126; Ssu-pu pei-yao ed., c. 3, pp. 10ᵃ–11ᵃ.

Early in the morning I step on my chariot
And, as I set out, feel myself to be far, far off.
The birds twitter to welcome the new year;
The gentle breeze wafts the goodness of the earth.

The cold bamboos skirt the deserted path;
The place, but sparsely inhabited, seems distant.
It was in such a mood that the weeding old recluse
Turned his back on the disciple and the world.[1]

These rustic thoughts I conceal from the wise and prudent,
So slender my stake in farming, so prodigious my
                                        clumsy efforts.

II

The Great Sage has said[2] for all time—
'Let truth, not food, be your prime consideration!'
I dare not emulate the austerity behind this teaching;
Rather than go hungry, I would gladly turn farmer:

To hold a plough and attend to seasonable duties,
Then with a cheerful countenance to encourage cultivation
And, when the wind from the Lake sweeps the plains,
To feel, like the waving corn, refreshed and animated;

[1] 'Tzu-lu, following the Master, happened to fall behind, when he met an old man, carrying across his shoulder on a staff a basket for weeds. Tzu-lu said to him, "Have you seen my master, sir?" The old man replied, "Your four limbs are unaccustomed to toil; you cannot distinguish the five kinds of grain – who is your master?" With this he planted his staff in the ground, and proceeded to weed. Tzu-lu joined his hands across his breast, and stood before him. The old man kept Tzu-lu to pass the night in his house, killed a fowl, prepared millet, and feasted him. He also introduced to him his two sons. Next day, Tzu-lu went on his way, and reported his adventure. The Master said, "He is a recluse", and sent Tzu-lu back to see him again, but when he got to the place, the old man was gone.' (*Analects*, Legge, xviii, viii, 1–4)

[2] 'The Master said, "The object of the superior man is truth. Food is not his object. There is plowing; even in that there is sometimes want. So with learning – emolument may be found in it. The superior man is anxious lest he should not get truth; he is not anxious lest poverty should come upon him".' (*Analects*, Legge, xv. xxxi). The 'posthaste travellers inquiring the way' is a reference to the disciple Tzu-lu being sent by Confucius to find out the way to the ford from the two hermits, Ch'ang-tsu and Chieh-ni, who were working in the fields. (*Analects*, Legge, xviii. vi)

With no thought of the harvest's abundance still to come,
To derive from the scene before me perennial joy,
For the ploughman takes his well-earned rest,
Unmolested by post-haste travellers inquiring the way;

At sundown when they all return from the day's toil,
To offer flasks of gruel to the nearest neighbours
And, left alone, to declaim verses before shutting my gate.
A farmer's life? One's lot could be worse!

An Excursion to Slanting Stream[1]
(401)

On the fifth of the first month in *hsin-ch'ou* year (401), the
weather being clear and mild and the scenery invested with a
tranquil beauty, I set out with two or three village friends on
an excursion to Slanting Stream. We stood by the river and
gazed at Wall Mount in the distance. The bream and the carp
leapt out of the water, their scales shining in the evening sun.
The gulls were flying about in the gentle breezes. As for Lu-
shan, the Southern Mountain, which has been celebrated from
olden times, we would not venture to praise it again. Wall
Mount is, however, an island peak, a lone eminence, before
which we recalled its namesake Mountain Wall in the Kunlun
range inhabited by immortals. Not satisfied with lingering in
the presence of a hill with a hallowed name, we each wrote a
poem lamenting the fleeting of time and the transience of our
own lives, adding also the year and the locality, as a record of
that day.

Five days have passed since the commencement of the year:
In my life, activity is giving way to rest,
Struck with which sobering thought
This very morning I set off on an excursion.

[1] p. 60; Ssu-pu pei-yao ed., c. 2, pp. 5ᵇ–6ᵃ. Slanting Stream (Hsieh
ch'uan), it would appear from the poem, was a river flowing past
Wall Mount in Singtze ('Meteorite County') on the west bank of
Poyang Lake. Wall Mount (Ts'eng-ch'eng), which has the same
name as a mountain wall in the Kunlun range in Tibet, seems to have
been an island on a marshy lake. The famous Lu-shan ('Mount Lu')
is situated to the north of Wall Mount.

The air is mild, the skies an unclouded azure,
As we sit in a row along the rushing river.
Down the rapids glide the streaked bream;
The screaming gulls flap their wings above the silent valley.

Our eyes rove aimlessly over the marshy lake
Until they rest on Wall Mount in the distance:
Though less magical than the enchanted Kunlun,
In its solitary eminence it has an air of majesty.

I lift the jug and motion my friends to take their places:
I fill the cups and drink to their health.
For who can tell the future—
Whether we might again re-live this moment?

Warmed by the drink, we let loose our hidden longings,
Relieved of the burden of the history of all the dynasties,
Making merry today while we still may,
Oblivious of the cares of the morrow.

The Alternation of the Seasons[1]

The Alternation of the Seasons: a poem about a walk in the
countryside in the last month of spring. The scenery being in
harmony with the warm weather, clad in new robes in ac-
cordance with ancient custom,[2] I sallied forth with for com-
panion only my shadow; and in my lone walk, joy and pensive
sadness intermingled in my heart.

The harmonious alternation of the seasons
Brings forth this sweet spring morning.
Having arrayed myself in the correct robes,
I set out for the fields in the east.

---

[1] pp. 6–7; Ssu-pu pei-yao ed., c. 1, pp. 2a–b.
[2] 'Last of all, the Master asked Tseng Hsi, "Tien, what are your
wishes?" Tien then said, "In this, the last month of spring, with the
dress of the season all complete, along with five or six young men
who have assumed the cap, and six or seven boys, I would wash in the
Yi, enjoy the breeze among the rain altars, and return home singing."
The Master heaved a sigh and said, "I give my approval to Tien".'
(*Analects*, Legge, xi. xxv, 7)

The hills have shed their last wintry haze
But a thin layer of clouds overspreads heaven's vault;
And a breeze from the south
Fans the growing corn.

In the broad, shallow stream
I rinse my mouth, then wash my feet.
I admire the distant prospect,
Joy welling up in my heart with each fresh gaze.
Men have a saying—
'He is easily content who follows his own bent':
Thus I drain this goblet
And delight in my own happiness.

My eyes alight upon the flowing current
And I think of that river of yore, the clear Yi,
Of the young men and boys who were fellow students,
Who after bathing there returned home singing.
I love such peaceful serenity,
For which I long both day and night.
But alas, they were of a different age,
So ancient as to be beyond recapture!

But indeed, morning or evening,
I find repose in my hut and garden,
Where the flowers and the herbs are separately bedded
And trees and bamboos both cast their shade.
Sustained by the throbbing guitar laid across my couch
And a jug half filled with unstrained wine,
Though I may not live in the golden age of the
                                        Yellow Emperor,
I still have the right of lamenting its passing.

South Village[1]

I

Earlier I meant to make my home in South Village —
Not that I took a fancy to the houses there,
But its dwellers were known as men of an unworldly stamp,
With whom it would be a pleasure to pass a morning
                                                    or evening.

Such, for years, was no more than my intention:
Today I find myself one of its inhabitants,
Housed, it is true, in a hut, primitive and narrow,
Though with room enough to spread out our beds and mats,

Where constantly we receive our good neighbours,
With whom I argue aloud about bygone days
Or read some masterly essay with keen enjoyment,
Interrupted only by enthusiastic analytical comments.

II

Spring and autumn bring many fine days,
On which I climb the heights and recite new poems;
And when I pass my neighbours at their gate,
We exchange greetings and I accept the wine they proffer.

After working on the land, we retire to our own dwellings;
Then, being at leisure, we desire one another's company;
So disposed, I throw on a coat to visit them,
And our talk and laughter continue endlessly.

This is the good life, more exciting than I can endure!
Let me, then, adopt no other,
Still exerting myself to supply the needs of food and clothing,
Confident that honest ploughing is a sure investment!

[1] p. 84; Ssu-pu pei-yao ed., c. 2, pp. 12a–b.

Hsieh Ling-yün

o

Hsieh Ling-yün

(385–433)

In the final years of the Eastern Tsin dynasty, no figure was more brilliant and dazzling than Hsieh Ling-yün, courtier and poet. He was born in the third year of the decisive victory over the Ti invaders (known as the 'Former Ch'in') by his grandfather Hsieh Hsüan, who in consequence was made Duke of K'ang-lo, a title Hsieh Ling-yün was to inherit. On his mother's side, he had as great uncle Wang Hsien-chih, the calligrapher, and would thus seem to be descended from Wang Hsi-chih.[1] The Wang and the Hsieh were the two leading families of the realm, so that no one was more fortunate in his birth than our poet. Since, however, Hsieh's father, who died early, was a dullard, our poet as an infant surprised his grandfather with his unusual intelligence. Of Hsieh's childhood little is known. To avert some unforeseen disaster from the favoured son, the family entrusted the boy at an early age to the care of a Buddhist monk, Tu-ming, who brought him up in Ch'ien-t'ang (i.e., Hangchow), some ninety kilometres north-west of their home. We may be certain that the West Lake and its surrounding hills impressed themselves on Hsieh even then. He probably read as diligently in the monastery as he would have done at home. And Buddhism became a subject of life-long interest.

In 399 Hsieh returned to the family estate at Shih-ning in Kuei-chi prefecture, where he had been born. Shih-ning (modern Shanyu in Chekiang Province) was situated to the east of the Kuei-chi Mountains, and the estate, planned and laid out by his grandfather, who had chosen the site because of its beautiful and secluded setting, comprised a northern and a southern hill, each with precipices and cascading streams,

[1] For Wang Hsi-chih, see 'General Introduction' *supra*.

separated by a lake. The family inhabited the northern hill, which had carefully sited gardens and orchards, terraces and walks, houses and ornate pavilions, all enjoying the best views, natural and artificial. The southern hill was left in a wilder state, later to be improved and built on by Hsieh himself. There were fields also and an abundance of crops at harvest time. The varieties of trees, bamboos, herbs delectable and medicinal, fruit, birds and beasts are catalogued in a composition in rhymed prose by Hsieh 'Dwelling among the Hills' (Shan-chü fu'[1]). Thus, until the age of fourteen or fifteen, Hsieh had known only the most beautiful surroundings.

A local uprising, which soon turned into a full-scale rebellion lasting four years, now caused those of the Hsieh family who were living in the country to flee to the capital Chien-k'ang (i.e., Nanking), where they had their official residence in Dark Robe Lane, haunted by swallows and probably originally named after the birds. In an age much given to luxury and display, the Hsieh house was among the most luxurious of establishments, and young Hsieh became a leader of fashion in dress and equipage. His talents in calligraphy and painting, in conversation and disputation, in prose and verse composition, together with his early succession to the ducal title and fief of three thousand households, made him the most admired figure of the time. A distinguished career in the family tradition seemed the only prospect before him.

But the fortunes of the dynasty, which his ancestors and especially his grandfather had upheld, were now on the wane. The uprising in Chekiang had been quelled, but Liu Yü, the general who had defeated the rebels, himself became a menace to the throne. The old families, sensing danger, allied themselves to a rival general, Liu I, whom our poet served as aide-de-camp and in other capacities almost continuously from 405 to 412. Being in active service entailed a certain amount of travelling, and in 411–12 Hsieh probably spent some time in Hsün-yang (i.e., Kiukiang), the prefectural town of T'ao Yüan-ming's Ch'ai-sang. Liu Yü, however, struck back in the

[1] The imperfectly preserved text of 'Shan-chü fu', complete with the poet's own annotation, may be found in Hsieh's official biography in *Sung shu*, c. 67.

autumn of 412, and both Liu I and Hsieh Hun, the leading member of the Hsieh clan, were executed. In effect, Liu Yü was now ruler of the Eastern Tsin empire; Hsieh Ling-yün and his faction were doomed.

Nevertheless, both sides continued their manoeuvres. Our poet, who was then twenty-seven, was far from adroit, but still well-connected and influential, and it suited Liu Yü's purpose that Hsieh should occupy various posts in the ensuing years. When, however, in 420 Liu Yü proclaimed himself Emperor of a new dynasty—'Sung', generally referred to as 'Liu Sung'—Hsieh was deprived of the rank of duke and made a marquis enjoying a fief of only five hundred households. As a counter-move, Hsieh and his friends attached themselves to one of their new ruler's sons, the Prince of Lu-ling, who was only in his early teens but already showed literary leanings and political ambitions. In 422 the new Emperor died and was succeeded by another prince. The Prince of Lu-ling was sent away from the capital and Hsieh appointed (in effect, banished) to the then remote prefecture of Yung-chia (i.e., Wenchow in Chekiang Province), noted for its hills and streams. It was the beginning of a creative phase, in which Hsieh left his political activities behind and devoted himself to the composing of verse.

After a journey up the Fuchun river and by land through some of the loveliest scenery in China, Hsieh reached Yung-chia in the autumn of 422. As Prefect, he modelled himself on certain worthies holding similar posts in the Han dynasty, whose creed in government had been non-activity and who had been able to afford to be occasionally ill without the fear of a piling up of litigation papers. Thus Hsieh roamed the hills all over his prefecture, and the scenery of Yung-chia is best left to his own account in the poems. There were, in fact, no mountains of very great height, but it was the unusual shapes of hills and the strange groupings of peaks and precipices—the picturesque even more than the sublime—that appealed to Chinese eyes. Yung-chia had the further advantage of being on the coast, the prefectural town—here referred to by its later name Wenchow—being on the south bank of the Yung-chia river, also known as the Ou, at its mouth.

In the autumn of 423, after holding office for a year, Hsieh resigned on grounds of health and returned to Shih-ning, where the southern hill, hitherto uncultivated, occupied much of his attention. As in Yung-chia, he also went on long tramps, accompanied by scores of servants as if on some expedition, often cutting their way through the trees and undergrowth. Here, too, he started a fashion, in wooden boots of his own invention with adjustable and removable spikes to facilitate ascent and descent. But the hill and lake scenery continued to inspire him, and his poems were transcribed and read all over the capital. In particular, the lake provided light effects caught by Hsieh as by no poet since. And the Shih-ning poems supplement the Yung-chia poems as Hsieh Ling-yün's enduring achievement.

The last ten years of Hsieh's life were dogged by misfortune. On the political scene, events moved with surprising speed. In 424, the Prince of Lu-ling was murdered, followed soon by the deposition and murder of the Emperor. Another prince ascended the throne and in 426 sent for Hsieh, who unwisely accepted office. He soon found himself relegated to a purely passive role, an ornament at court and a token of allegiance, and departed from the capital after two years, thoroughly disgruntled. Hsieh was now a marked man. In 430, the Prefect of Kuei-chi, an implacable enemy, accused him of treason. Hsieh hurried to the capital to plead his innocence before the Emperor, whereupon he was posted in 431 to Linchwan (i.e., Fuchow in Kiangsi Province), only to be impeached a year later for gross neglect of duty. He was then banished to Kwangchow (i.e., Canton), where in 433 on a flimsy pretext our poet was ordered to be executed. Hsieh met his end by writing a poem[1] containing the lines:

In the cause of my principles, I now lay down my life;

Alas, that I may not attain extinction on some hill-top!

In 'Reading in My Study', which may serve as an introduction to Hsieh's Yung-chia poems, the poet ponders the choice between the court, to which he by right belonged but where life was perilous, and the wild wastes, where he was safe but uncomfortable. The poem was written in the spring of 423,

[1] 'On the Point of Death', Huang, p. 115.

when Hsieh was in poor health and the birds were hopping about in the little frequented courtyard of his empty office. The classic pose, assumed by all later literary men, of the local official whose heart is among the hills, originates from this poem.

In 'An Evening Walk to Archers' Hall', the four memorable descriptive lines, ll. 3–6, show a keen awareness of the tone and gradation of colours. The significance of the 'bosom friends' (l. 12) is political, as is also that of the 'distant friends' in 'A Visit to South Pavilion'.

The first eight lines of 'Ascending Blue Screen Mountain', which re-enact the experience of mountain-climbing, have had a lasting influence on Chinese landscape poetry. For the climber has need of a stick and provisions, and is usually in search of some quiet or hallowed spot; in the south, he would take a boat for the first stage of his journey; and when he begins his ascent, he would be confronted by a stream in some hollow valley, clusters of bamboos, woods in the distance, a winding torrent.

In 'Stone Cave Mount', the sense of motion of one travelling in a speeding boat is one of Hsieh's additions to Chinese poetry.

'Solitary Island' on the Yung-chia river evokes in its lone splendour the habitation of the immortals, although in its isolation it would seem to mirror the poet himself.

In its neatness and compression, 'Ascending Cone Hill facing the sea' anticipates the T'ang poets. Its lines about the sea are of particular interest, as is also 'View of the sea from a hill on the coast', written early in the lunar year of 423, from which only four lines are translated.

In 'Sailing on the high seas after my visit to Red Rock', the unladen vessel pitching and rearing on the surging seas may be regarded as the poet's symbol of his own restlessness of spirit and boundless ambition. The experience itself was doubtless satisfying to him: he had reached the end of the world, and when he speaks of 'giving way to one's true nature', he seems to have found some degree of fulfilment.

Hsieh, unlike T'ao Yüan-ming, was one of those who consciously aimed at identification of the self with the cosmos.

Thus we find in 'Ascending Blue Screen Mountain':
> When one calmly commits the self to that
>
>   all-embracing unity,
> With knowledge and serenity aiding each
>
>   other's increase —
> A first step to restoring nature's primal condition;

and in 'A Visit to Solitary Island':
> A manifestation of divinity, to which none
>
>   have responded —
>
> . . . .
> This island renews my faith in the attainment
>
>   of infinite longevity.

To be sure, there is occasionally a note of exasperation with such abstract teachings, as in 'An Evening Walk to Archers' Hall':
> Casting aside arid doctrines like 'merging the self
>
>   in the universe';

but, in general, Hsieh gives the impression of having attained, in his ecstatic moments, that consonance with the cosmic principle sought by himself and others, as in 'Stone Cave Mount':

> The very hill, I at once knew, from which mortals
>
>   may ascend into heaven.
>
> So I look upon this sacred mount long in hiding
> As a hermit friend with whom to share my
>
>   intimate thoughts.

And the conceit of his being united with the hill is kept up by the presence of a mimosa tree, whose name also means 'joyful union'. In 'Ascending Stone Drum Hill', nature is regarded as a solace in the absence of friends. And we find in 'Stopping at White Sand Bank Pavilion':
> And spring and my heart seem that moment at one,

where the conceit hinges on the twisting of a phrase in *Ch'u tz'u.*

It will readily be seen that Hsieh's didactic concluding lines, in which he sets forth his doctrine, seldom fit the body of the poem. His skill as a poet is at fault, not the whole-heartedness of his response to nature. For he was fond of casuistry and disputation; and he wrote, not to please, but to be admired, so that his poems tend to be brilliant rather than harmonious compositions.[1] Basing his descriptions on close, personal observation, he fashions in his poems scattered and disparate elements into a unified, animated landscape. In this process, the poet's feeling or mood may colour a given scene and impose upon it a certain order; actual, observed details may be transformed by an arresting word or phrase into extravagant conceits; and, above all, a pictorial symmetry or balance may be maintained through the use of parallelism. This elaborate artifice has its triumphs, but may also relapse into awkward mannerisms and wilful obscurity. But without the over-all vision of a dynamic universe and a keen eye for form and colour, no amount of artistry would have enabled Hsieh to create the Chinese landscape poem.

For my translations I have followed in the main the text in Su Hsiao-hsüeh (ed.), *Hsieh Ling-yün shih hsüan*, Ku-tien 1957, but have also used Huang Chieh (ed.), *Hsieh K'ang-lo shih chu*, Jen-min 1958. In the footnotes, the two editions are referred to as 'Su' and 'Huang' respectively.

Reading in My Study[2]

Amidst the magnificent splendour of the capital,
I still cherished the lonely hills and ravines;
Now I am back among the streams and mountains,
My solitary disposition approves the sequestered scene.

Unmolested by contentious litigants in my empty office,
So quiet, the courtyard hums with the singing of birds,
Often ailing or convalescing, I have abundant leisure,
Which I devote to the writing of prose or verse.

To give scope to my ambitions, I survey times past

                        and present,
My prolonged reading being relieved by occasional jesting

---

[1] Hsieh's poetry is discussed in Chung Yung, 'The Grading of Five Poets' and Yen Yü, 'Memorable Lines in T'ao and Hsieh' in Volume III of this series.
[2] Su, pp. 59–60; Huang, p. 117.

At the expense of the ancient hermits toiling on the land
Or the slippery career of the soldier-scholar-courtier.[1]

For carrying a halberd all day fatigues body and mind,
And tilling the soil is unqualified drudgery.
Each mode of living has some inherent defect:
The wise adapt their aims to the conditions of their lives.

An Evening Walk to Archers' Hall[2]

As I turn my steps out of Wenchow's west gate,
I fix my gaze on the hills in the distance—
A screen of jutting peaks descending in multiple precipices,
Their blue-green fading in the misty twilight—

Hills bright with red maple leaves on frosty mornings,
Whose evening haze is shot through by golden sunbeams.
To measure my own past, what sorrows weigh upon me!
As to the future, already my mood colours my outlook!

The captive doe pines for its missing mate;
The stray bird regains its woodland shelter.
If attachment in mere creatures arouses compassion,
How much more, then, the parting from bosom friends?

From the mirror peers a face with greying temples;
The belt reveals my tight-fitting robe as too loose.
Casting aside arid doctrines like 'merging the self
                                        in the universe',
I confide my lone melancholy to my plaintive guitar.

---

[1] The reference is to Yang Hsiung (53 B.C.–A.D. 18), who had held for a time the position of halberd-bearer at court. During the usurper Wang Mang's reign, Yang Hsuing feared for his life and leapt out of an upper-floor window in one of the imperial libraries to escape arrest, thereby nearly killing himself.

[2] Su, p. 32; Huang, p. 34. Archers' Hall was in the outskirts of Wenchow. The title, which is ambiguous, is here taken to mean an evening walk to, rather than from, Archers' Hall. It is at least possible that the title was originally: 'An Evening Walk from the West Gate to Archers' Hall' ('Wan ch'u hsi-ch'eng wang she-t'ang'), and inadvertently shortened (to 'Wan ch'u hsi she-t'ang', as it now stands).

Ascending Blue Screen Mountain[1]

I set out with provisions and a stick in hand
On an arduous climb in search of a quiet retreat.
The boat carries me upstream; with the path turning sharply,
I step ashore and find fresh cause for wonder:

The rippling waves shimmering with a faint, cold light,
The fluttering bamboos with glassy, frost-covered stems,
The winding torrent playing hide-and-seek with me,
And beyond the far woods, a solid wall of precipices.

That glowing orb—is it the rising moon?
Or the setting sun? Do I face west or east?
Walking night and day, I confuse dawn with dusk,
Being hemmed in on all sides, in light as in darkness.

Two hexagrams[2] illumine my situation—'Worms', Top,
                                   'exempt from the service of princes';
'Treading', Second, 'Lucky is the hermit's even course'.
To be sure, I do tread the hermit's course,
But the lofty spirit is harder to sustain.

There is no room for 'Yea' or 'Nay'
When one calmly commits the self to that all-embracing unity,
With knowledge and serenity aiding each other's increase—
A first step to restoring nature's primal condition.

---

[1] Su, p. 34; Huang, pp. 48-9.
[2] 'xviii. The Ku Hexagram . . . 6. The sixth line, undivided, shows us one who does not serve either king or feudal lord, but in a lofty spirit prefers to attend to his own affairs.

x. The Li Hexagram . . . 2. The second line, undivided, shows its subject treading the path that is level and easy; a quiet and solitary man, to whom, if he be firm and correct, there will be good fortune.' (Legge, *The Ifi King*, Text, Section 1)

Peaks' Gateway[1]

In the Han, non-activity was the art of government:
The perfect prefect was one who exerted himself least.
In such a role one might be sent to any province;
The speckless tradition, not the locality, was the consideration.

It was my fortune to descend on this southern region,
Whose people are wholly devoid of the spirit of strife;
Thus I pace the quiet and desolate sea-shore
Or think unearthly thoughts in my uncluttered office.

In the first month of winter with my companions
I tour on a morning the countryside I so delight in.
A hundred prospects open out before me:
A thousand hills each different in shape,

The forbidding sheerness of the three peaks,
The swift current of the twin rivers,
On which fishermen and traders ply their boats
Past silhouettes of trees and woodcutters in the setting sun.

Though none may lay claim to complete happiness,
He is happy who would not diverge from his aims.

[1] Su, pp. 36–7; Huang, p. 50. Ling-men shan is described as a hill with a fissure in the middle dividing it into neat halves, so that from a distance one gains the impression of a gateway between two peaks; from the 'three peaks' in 1.13 one would infer that there was another peak in the distance. The location of the hill is uncertain, being in one account twenty-five and in another account forty kilometres south of Wenchow.

A Visit to South Pavilion[1]

Spring draws near its end with this fine and clear evening;
The clouds have dispersed, the sun speeds westwards.
By the woods there is a freshness in the air,
Over the hill, the remaining half of a red disc.

Distressed by days of incessant downpour,
From this pavilion I rejoice in the view of the town's outskirts.
The orchids by the pond have overspread the path
And the lotus flowers are in their first flush.

Even before we have enjoyed spring to the full,
Summer is already round the corner.
How the changing scene has affected my spirits!
I see streaks of grey hair blown about in the breeze.

Music and banqueting may arrest the passage of time
But all too soon illness and decay are with us.
Even so will come autumn with its attendant floods,
When I hope to perch my shadow under my native cliffs.[2]

These thoughts I may share with no one in the present:
A few distant friends have long known and understood them.

[1] Su, pp. 49–50; Huang, pp. 37–8.
[2] ll. 15–16 hint at Hsieh's plan of returning to Shih-ning in the autumn, the poem being written in late spring 423.

Stopping at White Sand Bank Pavilion[1]

Trailing my robes, I walk along the sandy embankment;
I halt my steps and enter this thatched shed.
Near by, a torrent washes heap upon heap of pebbles;
Scattered woods in the distance skirt the hills,
Encircled by that indefinable blue-green haze.
A fisherman suddenly bursts into song;
Holding on to a creeper, I listen under a moss-grown cliff,
And spring and my heart[2] seem that moment at one.
The yellow birds flit about[3] and alight on the oak tree,
The belling deer browse on the celery of the meadows,[4]
The one mocking the live burial of good men mourned by all,
The other recalling the prince feasting and rewarding
                                                    his nobles.

Thus glory and decay exist in rotation;
Success and failure may each bring joy or sorrow.
Far better to be always indifferent to worldly fortunes,
Holding fast to one's original simplicity in all one's actions!

[1] Su, p. 47; Huang, pp. 41–2. White Sand Bank Pavilion, which was on the south bank of the Nan river, was over forty kilometres north-west of Wenchow. The allusions to the Book of Poetry, noted below, contain personal references.

[2] 'spring and my heart': the phrase is probably derived from the penultimate line of 'The Invocation of the Soul' in *Ch'u tz'u*, c. 9:
    My eye scans the horizon and my spring-filled heart is touched.

[3] See Legge, *The Book of Poetry*, Part I, XI. vi:
    1. They flit about, the yellow birds, / And rest upon the jujubes find. / Who buried were in duke Muh's grave / Alive to awful death consigned? / . . . / Why thus destroy our noblest men, / To thee we cry, O azure Heaven! / To save Yen-seih from death, we would / A hundred lives have freely given.

[4] See *The Book of Poetry*, Part II, I. i:
    1. With sounds of happiness the deer / Browse on the celery of the meads. / A nobler feast is furnished here, / With guests renowned for noble deeds. / The lutes are struck; the organ blows, / Till all its tongues in movement heave. / Each basket loaded stands, and shows / The precious gifts the guests receive. / . . .

Stone Cave Mount[1]

This clear dawn I go in quest of a secret marvel.
The boat speeds past many a wooded field,
Lush reeds and rushes, an islet overgrown with orchids;
Imposing green hills loom in the distance.

Stone Cave Mount rises crown-like above the tree-tops,
With a shining cataract near its peak.
The river has flowed on in obscurity for a millennium;
And the hill itself was prominent in ancient times,

Though now not heard of by the villagers,
And the woodcutters are debarred from its airy heights.
It stands aloof and commands no extensive views,
The very hill, I at once knew, from which mortals may
                                    ascend into heaven.

So I look upon this sacred mount long in hiding
As a hermit friend with whom to share my intimate thoughts.
The mimosa tree stoops to prevent my speaking,
And I pluck its blossoms and stroke its branches.[2]

A Visit to Solitary Island on the Yung-chia River[3]

Being sated with the sights south of the Yung-chia,
Having long neglected the hills to its north,
Ever eager to see new places, I follow the most devious routes
In search of strange scenery, which seems yet to elude me.

Cleaving the current, we steer straight across the river
And meet head-on the lone island that graces the mid stream,
Shone upon by the glorious sun with a train of luminous clouds,
Poised between an azure sky and clear, blue waters:

[1] Su, p. 95; Huang, p. 78. I am presuming the subject of this poem to be the Shih-shih shan, regarded as a sacred hill, situated over a hundred *li* to the north-west of Wenchow. There is another Shih-shih shan in the vicinity of Hsieh's home at Shih-ning.

[2] Ho-huan, the name of the mimosa tree, also means 'happy union' i.e., of the poet and the hill he had sought out.

[3] Su, p. 54; Huang, p. 47. Solitary Island is immediately north of Wenchow.

A manifestation of divinity, to which none have responded —
And if inhabited by immortals, they are unknown to men —
Suggestive of the magical Kunlun, home of the gods,
And likewise remote from the cares of the world.

This island renews my faith in the attainment of
                                      infinite longevity,
And I shall endeavour at least to live out my natural span.

Ascending Stone Drum Hill[1]

The traveller's heart is burdened with long-standing grief —
His sorrows form the links of a chain —
His native village being far, far away,
With rivers and hilly country in between.

Alone, without congenial company in springtime,
He gives vent to his feelings by climbing mountains.
Since unfulfilled longings preclude present happiness,
May his brooding melancholy yet find solace!

His eye roves over the wide expanse to the left;
He turns and peers into the deep ravine on the right:
When the sun sets, the torrent quickens
And the gathering clouds add layers to the peaks and ridges.

Fragrant plants and sweet herbs rejoice alike in
                                     spring's coming;
The lentil and duckweed put forth new leaves.
The wanderer plucks a flower, which affords him no relief;
He plays on the lute, but finds the sounds discordant.

Dateless the appointed time of his recall,
And watching and waiting bring no comfort!

[1] Su, p. 41; Huang, p. 43. Shih-ku shan ('Stone Drum Hill') is an island on the Yung-chia river forty *li* to the west of Wenchow. At the top of it was a hollow stone, which, when beaten upon, reverberated like a drum.

*Ascending Cone Hill facing the sea
during a tour of inspection of the land*[1]

The hardships of travel find few compensations,
Of which one is a view of the sea by morning.
Who can tell me where the flood of waves subsides
Or what lands lie east of the main?

Strains of a lotus-root picker's song quiver in the wind;
I see her now, with eyebrows knit like that ancient beauty.[2]
Having visited many a green sandy islet,
Today I ascend a cinnabar red hill.

View of the sea from a hill on the coast[3]

Spring's beginning marks the start of the year;
The bright sun in its splendour proclaims a new day:
I purge my melancholy and prepare myself for joy
By gazing upon the sea, in which I drown my sorrows.

. . . .

[1] Su, p. 58; Huang, pp. 42–3. P'an-yü shan ('Cone Hill') is on the north bank of the mouth of the Yung-chia about twenty kilometres east of Wenchow.

[2] The ancient beauty with the knitted eyebrows: Hsi Shih, who afterwards brought about the destruction of the Wu kingdom. Certainly in later tradition, Hsi Shih sang lotus-pickers' songs.

[3] Su, p. 39; Huang, p. 49. The poem as a whole is too allusive— being almost wholly dependent on *Ch'u tz'u* for its themes and diction—to convey much information about the actual scene. Of the four opening lines here rendered, the first three are entirely derivative. The reference to the sea is, however, Hsieh's own.

Sailing on the high seas after my visit to Red Rock[1]

In early summer the heat is still soothing
Nor are flowering plants all past their best.
Confined to the anchored boat from dawn to dusk,
I watch the changing sky, in turn cloudy, clear, overcast.
Of the strand and its scenery, I have had my fill:
To cross the seas still seems an adventure.

On a day when the river god has calmed the current
And the ruler of the waves recalled the billows,
Hoisting sail, we move out of the bay to catch scallops
And then, changing tack, fish for sea melons.
On the boundless surging sea,
The unladen vessel, now in its element, pitches and
                                         rears with ease.

Though some genuinely shun rank and office,
Others make a pretence of the anchorite's life.
To seek fame through avoiding the world is no fulfilment:
By giving way to one's nature, one dissolves
                                         worldly attachments.
Let me, then, follow the good advice of the ancients
And seek self-preservation through self-realisation!

[1] Su, pp. 51–2; Huang, p. 45.

Wang Wei

O

Wang Wei
(701–61)

Wang Wei was one of the most gifted of men: a consummate musician at a time—in the T'ang dynasty—when music flourished in China, one of the great masters of Chinese painting, a poet among the first rank in the golden age of Chinese poetry. The combination was not uncommon, but the degree of attainment unusual. Of Wang Wei as a musician only anecdotes remain. In the sphere of painting, no authentic specimen of his brush seems to have survived, although painters from the Sung to the Ming have gratefully acknowledged his influence. His poems, however, are preserved in a corpus first edited by his younger brother Wang Chin at the command of the Emperor.

For the T'ang was an era of enlightened rule and liberal patronage, and Wang Wei and indeed his brother, too, won recognition through their talents alone. The family, for generations middle-ranking officials, were originally from Kihsien in the prefecture of Taiyuan (in Shansi Province), where our poet was born, but moved in his father's time to P'u-chou (i.e., Yungtsi, also in Shansi). Wang Wei was precocious, and even his juvenilia have withstood the test of time. From the age of fourteen we find him more or less continuously in the capital Ch'ang-an (modern Sian in Shensi Province), which we might regard as his home. Though he did not always occupy an official position, from the age of nineteen he was a social celebrity.

Tradition has it that Prince Ch'i, who knew Wang's worth, tried to secure for him the patronage of the Princess Royal. At a banquet in honour of the Princess, the handsome and graceful Wang, disguised as a musician in the Prince's train, astonished the company by playing on the lute one of his own compositions. The Princess's curiosity being aroused, Wang was then told to present her with a manuscript roll containing ten of his poems. The delighted Princess soon discovered that she already knew the poems, some of them being her favourite poems. And, charmed with their young author, she bestirred herself from that moment to advance him.

Thus at the age of twenty Wang became Deputy Master of Music. The appointment terminated abruptly a few months later when he was sent off—according to tradition, Wang took part in a lion dance, which was against etiquette—to a post at Chi-chou (in Shantung Province, the site of the town, which was over forty kilometres to the south-west of Tsinan, being now submerged by the Yellow River). It was a set-back in his career as an official, although it provided an op-portunity for travel: T'ai-shan, chief of the five Holy Mount-ains, was only about fifty kilometres from Chi-Chou; and from scattered references to the sea's shore in his poems, one would infer that he probably also saw the sea.

After serving in Chi-chou for a period, Wang quietly re-turned to the capital. No spectacular rise was to follow. Nevertheless, as musician, as painter and as calligrapher, he was much sought after. When in 728 Meng Hao-jan visited Ch'ang-an Wang entertained him; and in the title of a poem[1] by Meng, Wang is referred to as an Assistant Censor. Certainly he would seem to be in attendance at the palace with easy access to the Emperor Hsüan-tsung.

Wang, however, like other scholars of his time, cherished political ambitions. He was eager to serve under the upright and outspoken Chang Chiu-ling, who became Prime Minister in 734. At the age of thirty-three, Wang was made a Re-minder, a post within the central administration with duties similar to those of the censors, and he doubtless acquitted his responsibilities with conscientious zeal. For when, three years later, Chang left for Ching-chou (i.e., Kiangling in Hupeh Province), Wang expressed his regret in a moving poem,[2] full of gratitude for the kind favours he had received from Chang, who 'alone had cognisance of my abilities'. With the

[1] Hsiao, *Meng Hao-jan shih shuo*, p. 73.
[2] c. 7, p. 121.

departure of Chang Chiu-ling from the sphere of government, and the ascendancy of the shifty and crafty Li Lin-fu, Wang lost his relish for public affairs.

Thus, when in 737, having earlier reverted to the role of Assistant Censor, Wang was dispatched on a tour of the frontier to Liang-chou (i.e., Wuwei in Kansu Province), he accepted the invitation of the local commander to remain there and serve. And it was not until late in 738 or early in 739 that he returned to Ch'ang-an with a number of poems describing the frontier scene with the freshness of one accustomed to the densely populated central plains.

There was an otherworldly strain in Wang which came increasingly to the fore with the years. He had been brought up as a Buddhist by his mother, to whom he was utterly devoted, and the piety instilled in him in early childhood never abandoned him. While still in his twenties, he retreated for a time to Sung-shan (near Tengfeng in Honan Province), another of the Holy Mountains. This probably took place immediately after his return from Chi-chou. It was no more than a trial, at the end of which he again took part in mundane affairs.

Soon after his return from the north-west frontier in 738–9, Wang made another retreat, to the Chung-nan Mountains, about thirty-five kilometres south of Ch'ang-an. He was out of office and, following a pattern set by the lives of T'ao and Hsieh, considered the possibility of retirement. By Chinese count he was aged forty:

Middle age led my thoughts to the eternal:

Late in life I made my home below these mountains.

In fact, he was full of vitality and explored the Chung-nan and the neighbouring Lantien mountains with the joy of discovery. This phase of withdrawal probably lasted only about a year, but it gave him a foretaste of the secluded life which he was to lead five or six years hence. It was at this time that Wang found in P'ei Ti, who would be a dozen or so years his junior, a congenial companion, possessing literary gifts and a temperament akin to his own. P'ei, too, sought solitude in the Chung-nan Mountains, to whose memory he remained faithful in after years. For both friends, those mountains were

ever enduring in a world of change and vicissitudes, and the
main Chung-nan peak was almost the embodiment of eternity.

In 740–1, having resumed his duties at the Censorate,
Wang was sent on a tour of inspection to Hsiang-yang (i.e.,
Siangyang in Hupeh Province), where he narrowly missed
his friend Meng Hao-jan, who had died earlier in 740. From
742 Wang was continuously in the capital, serving also in the
Boards. He was now more than ever inclined to a life of
detachment and contemplation away from the press and bustle
of governmental affairs. As an artist, he had received sub-
stantial rewards over a score or more years, so that he could
afford to purchase a large estate to provide a permanent re-
treat for himself and a shrine for his mother's devotions. The
estate was ten kilometres south-west of Lantien, a town about
forty kilometres to the south-east of the capital. He was thus
able to repair to it at regular intervals. And when his mother
died in 747–8, his three-year period of mourning was also
spent there. Grief at her passing at first reduced him to a
near-skeleton—his wife had died much earlier, in 731—but
he recovered and was in office again by 751–2.

The acquisition, planning and laying out of the estate—
known as 'Wang-ch'uan' ('Wheel Stream') because at the
mouth of the gorge by which it was situated, the swift current
of the stream met another stream, as a result of which it
whirled round in eddies like so many spoked chariot wheels—
probably took place in the years 744–7. The estate had pre-
viously belonged to the poet Sung Chih-wen (c. 663–712),
but there had been a lapse of over thirty years between the
two owners. Gardens and Chinese houses decay rapidly, so
that we might presume all the twenty views of 'Wang-ch'uan'
to have been planned by Wang. The twenty poems by Wang
and the companion poems by P'ei Ti—together known as the
'Wang-ch'uan Poems'—would date from the second and
third year of the acquisition, when every prospect and vista,
every nook and recess, were in accordance with Wang's
fastidious taste. Though companion pieces are often dull, we
are fortunate to have the impressions of 'Wang-ch'uan' con-
tained in the poems by P'ei Ti, who had his own preferences,
and whose observations supplement Wang's.

When Wang re-emerged from his period of mourning, he again held various offices and probably concerned himself more than he had for some time with the conduct of affairs. But, at this point, the memory of Wang himself, as well as the historians who wrote his official biographies in the Old and New T'ang History, was blurred by the breaking out of the An Lu-shan rebellion, an upheaval which left the two capitals Ch'ang-an and Loyang in ruins, the empire in widespread chaos and our poet in deep disgrace. When the rebels entered Ch'ang-an in 756, Wang's desperate attempt to save himself by destroying his voice proved ineffectual. They held him captive, sent him to Loyang, and conferred a rebel title on him. When order was in some measure restored and a new T'ang emperor, Su-tsung, reinstated in Ch'ang-an in 757, Wang underwent a period of detention. He was redeemed, however, by the willingness of his brother Wang Chin, who, because of his valour in defending their native Taiyuan against the rebels, had been made Under Secretary of the Board of Punishments, to have his own rank reduced. Wang Wei, demoralised and broken in spirit, occupied himself with Buddhist activities from then on, though, in the very next year, 758, he was again appointed to offices and, in 759, made a Deputy Prime Minister, a position he held until his death in 761.

Chronologically, the translated poems form two groups: those dating from the year in the Chung-nan Mountains, which include also 'The Stone Temple in the Lantien Mountains'; and those dating from the early years at the estate. The latter are introduced by Wang's letter to P'ei Ti and by a poem of P'ei's which forms a link between the two groups. Next come two poems written in the first autumn at 'Wang-ch'uan' and the well-known 'Wang-ch'uan Poems'. Wang's visit to P'ei in Ch'ang-an is recorded in 'The Tower in P'ei Ti's House'. The early years at 'Wang-ch'uan' end with P'ei's departure from the capital, noted in two poems, in the second of which Wang laments the absence of his friend. Three other poems about 'Wang-ch'uan', probably dating from the 750s, are also included, two of them placed together under the title 'Returning to Wang-ch'uan in Spring'.

Of P'ei Ti's subsequent life, this much is certain: he per-
severed in his career and he persisted in the writing of verses.
For, when we next meet him in 760, he was host to Tu Fu at
Sintsing (about forty-five kilometres south-west of Chengtu
in Szechuan Province), a town in Shu-chou, of which P'ei was
Prefect, and together the two went up a hill to see a monastery,
where P'ei wrote a poem addressed to Wang Wei's brother,
Wang Chin, to which Tu added a companion poem.[1] A second
poem[2] of Tu's written during that visit was in accompaniment
of another poem by P'ei. In a third poem, probably dating
from the following year, addressed to P'ei,[3] Tu observes
that—

The throes of verse composition have made you thin.

Coming from Tu Fu, who himself worked unremittingly on
his poems, this was a compliment indeed. Few, however, of
P'ei's poems are preserved, and he is known in literary history
as the friend and follower of Wang Wei.

The estate seems to have been situated in a hidden valley or
ravine by the Wang-ch'uan river and gorge. According to the
local histories, a narrow cutting through the rocks leads from
the mouth of the gorge, where the traveller would step ashore
from his boat, across the mountains to a spacious valley; from
the other side of the valley a devious path leads to the ravine
which is the site of Wang Wei's estate. The ravine itself is
divided by its shape and contour into thirteen sections of un-
usual scenery. From the poems themselves we may conjec-
ture that at the end of the ravine one met the Wang-ch'uan
river again, shallow enough in those upper reaches to wade
through, though too steep and swift for any boat. Thus the
artfully contrived views of Wang's day rested largely on the
natural setting. Of the twenty sights, the most intriguing is
Old Wall Glen, where Wang had his house built in the shadow
of an old town wall—known as 'Meng-ch'eng'—about
which no one in the eighth century knew anything.

---

[1] Ch'iu Chao-ao (ed.), *Tu Shao-ling chi hsiang-chu*, c. 9, Wen-hsüeh
ku-chi ed., Vol. iv, p. 124. For Tu Fu's tribute to Wang Wei himself,
see 'On the Writing of Verse' in Volume iii of this series.
[2] Vol. iv, p. 133.
[3] Vol. iv, p. 134.

There would seem to be two hills on the estate, Hua-tzu-kang Ridge and Axe-leafed Bamboo Peak, both named after places celebrated by Hsieh Ling-yün. Additionally, there would be mounds and hillocks, including North and South Knoll separated by a lake, reminiscent of the northern and southern hills on Hsieh's estate. The mountains mentioned in the poems would be outside the grounds. In the adjoining valley would be hamlets and cultivated fields, including fields belonging to the estate. Thus though the situation of 'Wang-ch'uan' was a secluded one, Wang was not cut off from society, as he makes clear in some of the poems.

Wang Wei's relatively easy personal circumstances, the stability and prosperity of the times in which he passed most of his days, the unstudied poise of the social celebrity, his placid temperament, Buddhist piety and resignation have all contributed to the perfect calm and transparency of his poems. The predominant impressions they convey are tranquillity and harmony, reflecting order and concord in the universe. The scene or mood is seldom marred by an emphatic statement. The voice is never strident and the words, having carried a certain meaning, vanish into thin air. In this lightness of touch may be detected the hand of the artist who, by the acknowledge-ment of all, softened the harsh lines of solid landscapes in the earlier tradition into the graceful curves of his ink washes. For our poet seems to subsume his identity under the conventions of rural and landscape poetry set up by T'ao and Hsieh, namely, the lowly cottage, the cheerful farming neighbours, the fields, banks and furrows, the sowing, the self-imposed seclusion, on the one hand; the lake and hills, the bamboo grove and woods, mountain streams and precipices lit up by the setting sun or rising moon, the sense of adventure, on the other. And yet the man's personality emerges distinctly. One might almost say that the transparency of his personality is the poetic achievement of Wang Wei. Who else has succeeded in transmitting such moods of calmness, tranquillity and ease? The beauty and melodiousness, which are to be found every-where, seem almost an afterthought.

Wang's conception of landscape, as is obvious from the names of his hills and mounds, was derived from Hsieh.

Indeed 'Wang-ch'uan' must seem artificial if placed beside
Hsieh's Shih-ning with its natural advantages. But Wang
knew the limits of poetry in respect of description and, instead
of exact delineation of a given scene, as had been attempted by
Hsieh, brings about the intended effect by a few random
details, carelessly interspersed. The result would be a sketch
rather than a precise account, often containing colour or light
or sound effects which impress through their directness and
immediacy and through the very lack of emphasis. Thus,
although Wang tends to use the most generalised expressions,
his descriptive lines nevertheless leave an impression of sharp-
ness and clarity. Wang's response to nature may be described
as contemplative rather than impassioned, but he has endowed
what portion of nature he chose to represent with harmony
and serenity.

For my translations I have used Chao Tien-ch'eng(ed.),
Wang Yu-ch'eng chi chien-chu, Chung-hua 1961, and the *chüan*
and page references in the footnotes are to that edition. (For
the Ssu-pu pei-yao edition of the same work, the *chüan*
references are the same.)

Chung-nan Mountain[1]

Jade Emperor Mountain[2] stands watch over our
                                        celestial capital;
Its adjoining ridges reach out to the ocean's shore.
The enfolding white clouds, under one's gaze, turn into
                                        a noble crown;
The azure-tinted mists, when peered at, disappear into
                                        some cave.

Its middle peak bestrides more than one terrestrial region;
Each ravine is overhung by a different sky.
For a night's lodging for the lost traveller,
A woodcutter across the stream gives willing direction.

[1] c. 7, p. 124.
[2] T'ai-i shan ('Mountain of the Ruler of Heaven') is another name
for Chung-nan Mountain.

A Cottage at the foot of Chung-nan Mountain[1]

Middle age led my thoughts to the eternal:
Late in life I made my home below these mountains.

Guided by fancy, I would wander all alone,
Delighting secretly in my private explorations.

I would track a stream to its fountain-head
Or sit on a rock to watch the clouds gather at sunset,

And meeting by chance some aged woodsman,
Forget to return, enthralled by the rustic conversaion.

The Stone Temple in the Lantien Mountains[2]

The setting sun highlights the hills and the river,
On which my boat is adrift in the evening breeze.
Heedless of distance, intent on discovering new scenery,
I row upstream to trace the river's source.
Admiring from afar the tall, luxuriant woods,
I fear my course would lead no further,
When with a sudden turn the limpid stream
Veers towards the very hill I was heading for.

I leave my boat and carry a walking-stick,
And am rewarded by a sight that soon confronts me:
Five or four venerable monks
Taking their ease under the pine and fir trees,
Who chant their morning prayers before the wood sees
                                                    light of day
And sink into nocturnal meditation when the mountains
                                                    are still;
Their holy zeal they extend even to the cowherds,
But in the world's affairs they seek instruction from
                                                    the woodcutters.

Benighted, I make ready to sleep under the trees,
Burn incense and recline on a mat.

[1] c. 3, p. 35.
[2] c. 3, pp. 33–4.

A new fragrance arising from the torrent pervades my clothes,
And the ascending moon casts its rays on the precipice—
No more exploration tonight, lest indeed I lose my way!
At dawn I shall venture forth afresh
And bid farewell to the inhabitants of this lost valley,
Whom, guided by my own tracks, I may one day visit again.

Letter to P'ei Ti written in the Mountains[1]

[The letter dates from the winter (probably of 746) preced-
ing the spring in which P'ei left Ch'ang-an. From it we learn
how the 'Wang-ch'uan Poems'—by now completed—were
written. Many, at least, of the lines came to Wang and P'ei
on their walks, whether along the slopes or by some clear
stream. That Wang should find it necessary to justify his
interest in the hills and the countryside may seem strange to
us, but perhaps P'ei's 'unworldly cast of mind' was already
being subjected to other influences. Certainly P'ei's system-
atic study suggests preparation for a regular civil service
career.

The Pa, of which the Wang-ch'uan is a tributary, flows
past the town of Lantien northwards into the Wei river. Its
nearest point to Sian is about ten kilometres to the north-east
of the city. When Wang says that he 'was ferried across' the
Pa, he really means that he was carried upstream past Lantien
and up the Wang-ch'uan river to the mouth of the gorge.]

It being the last month of the year and the weather fine and
unexpectedly mild, these our old haunts were well worth
visiting. Since I knew that you were engaged in a systematic
re-reading of the classics, not wishing to disturb you, I set off
by myself for the mountains. After a short rest at Kan-p'ei
Temple, where I supped with the monk, I proceeded north-
wards and was ferried across the black stream of the Pa under
a silvery moon that illumined the outskirts of the city [Ch'ang-
an]. I ascended Hua-tzu-kang Ridge by night. Below, the
rippling waves of the Wang-ch'uan river danced with the
moonbeams. In the distance, the hills looked cold and bare,

[1] c. 18, p. 332.

although a fire here and there defined the shapes of trees and woods. In a winding lane a dog was barking furiously, the reverberation resembling a leopard's growl. And the noise of the villagers' threshing alternated with the sound of the temple bell.

At this moment I am seated by myself, with the servants hushed and out of sight. And my thoughts hark back to former days, when hand in hand we would walk along some mountain path to stop before a clear stream, composing verses as we went. It cannot now be long before spring. The plants and trees will put forth leaves and the hills will be seasonally clad in green for all to admire. Shoals of small, leaf-like white fish will leap out of the water, and the white gulls spread their wings. The grass on the river bank will be moist with dew, and the wheat fields echoing of a morning with the crowing of pheasants. Perhaps you will then be free to roam the hills with me? If I did not know your pure and unworldly cast of mind, I should not have presumed to ask you to join in this idle and useless activity, from which, however, one may derive deep interest and lasting satisfaction. Pray give the matter more than a passing thought. The dye-wood gatherers who will carry this are leaving, and I must close.

From the Mountain-dweller, Wang Wei

P'ei Ti: 'Reminiscences of Chung-nan Mountain while caught in the rain at Wang-ch'uan Gorge', and Wang Wei's accompanying poem[1]

P'EI

The rain has darkened our narrow sky;
The sandy shore has erased our rainbow.
The waters of the Wang-ch'uan flow on and on,
But where is ever enduring Chung-nan Mountain?

WANG

The current is swollen, the river has risen,
The rains of autumn have blotted out the skies.
Chung-nan Mountain, invisible and out of reach,
Remains where it was, encircled by white clouds.

[1] c. 13, p. 239.

Addressed to P'ei Ti from 'Wang-ch'uan'[1]

The deserted hills have turned a sombre green;
Summer's humming streams are now autumn torrents.
Leaning on my stick outside my cottage,
I hear the cicadas chirp in the evening breeze.

At the ferry, the red orb of the sun is sinking;
A lone column of smoke rises from the hamlet.
You will find me like the madman of Ch'u,[2] but
                                              inebriated as well,
Accosting you with a quaint old song before his hermitage.

Evening in Autumn among the Hills[3]

The rains have fallen. The hills are bare
On this clear autumn's evening.
Over the pines a moon has risen.
The stream is cascading on the rocks.
The bamboos are loud with the chatter of
                              returning washerwomen.
The lotus leaves sway before a lowered fishing-boat.
Green grass is everywhere for tired feet and eyes,
And even a fastidious sightseer will choose to linger.

[1] c. 7, p. 122. The poem would date from soon after Wang Wei took up residence at 'Wang-ch'uan'. P'ei would not have had an opportunity of visiting the estate, and our poet goes into raptures over his fancied role of hermit.

[2] See Analects XVIII. 5. There is also an allusion to T'ao Yüan-ming in the following line, which I have suppressed.

[3] c. 7, pp. 122–3. Like the previous poem, the epistle to P'ei Ti, this one would date from the first autumn of Wang Wei's residence at 'Wang-ch'uan'. Many, at least, of the 'sights' had not yet been properly laid out, and the estate was in a far less cultivated state than in the 'Wang-ch'uan Poems'.

'The Wang-ch'uan Poems'[1]

In my retreat in Wang-ch'uan ravine, the sights include Old
Wall Glen, Hua-tzu-kang Ridge, Apricot Pavilion, Axe-leafed
Bamboo Peak, the Deer Park, the Purple Magnolia Garden,
Dogwood Bank, Locust-tree Alley, Lake Pavilion, South
Knoll, Fair Lake, Willow Bank, Luan's Shoal, Gold Dust
Fountain, White Stone Shoal, North Knoll, Bamboo Grove
Pavilion, Magnolia Bank, the Lacquer Garden and the Pepper
Garden. Being at leisure in the company of P'ei Ti, I, and
then he too, wrote poems on every one of them, comprising
four lines each.

1) *Old Wall Glen*

WANG

A new dwelling at the mouth of an old wall:
Of the old trees, some ailing willows remain.
A vain thought—who will inhabit the place after me,
Even as I grieve for its previous celebrated owner?[2]

P'EI

He makes his home beneath an old wall
And time and again climbs up the old ramparts.
The old town is no longer there to be defended—
New men walk back and forth, oblivious of its ruins.

2) *Hua-tzu-kang Ridge*

WANG

The birds fly south in unending procession—
These hills again wear the colours of autumn—
As I make my way up the ridge and down again,
A feeling of deep sadness enwraps me.

P'EI

At sunset a wind rises from the pine woods;
Returning to the house, we find the dew thin, the
grass withered.
Our footsteps up the ridge have been erased by the clouds,
But still my sleeves seem to brush against the mountain's
autumnal green.

---

[1] c. 13, pp. 241–50.   [2] The poet Sung Chih-wen, who died in 712.

3) *Apricot Pavilion*
WANG

The beam is wood from the apricot tree,
The roof is sweet-smelling thatch,
And the clouds that invade its eaves
Dissolve in rain over the populated plains.

P'EI

Distant Apricot Pavilion,
Up which we daily climb,
Taking in Bamboo Peak and the Lake
As southward and then northward we gaze!

4) *Axe-leafed Bamboo Peak*
WANG

Pliant yet upright, these bamboos adorn slope and peak,
Their green leaves fluttering over an eddying stream,
Concealing the path to the hermitage
From even the sure-footed woodcutters.

P'EI

A mountain stream, now winding, now straight,
Skirts these bamboos, dense and impenetrable,
And blazes the trail to the next mountain,
Where, singing aloud, we look back with wonder at this peak.

5) *The Deer Park*
WANG

Not the shadow on a man on the deserted hill—
And yet one hears voices speaking;
Deep in the seclusion of the woods,
Stray shafts of the sun pick out the green moss.

P'EI

We visit the hill in the early evening
And think ourselves the only frequenters,
But the pine woods, dim and silent,
Reveal the neatly printed tracks of buck and doe.

6) *The Purple Magnolia Garden*
   WANG

The autumnal hills soak up the sloping rays;
The returning birds fly in pairs;
The hill-side blazons such sharply defined colours,
The evening mists have kept away.

   P'EI

As the sky deepens at sunset,
The birds so confuse the stream with their chirrup,
That it, and our path too, takes a strange turning,
Leading us with our thirst for new sights whither?

7) *Dogwood Bank*
   WANG

The berries are red and green—
The trees seem again in flower:
To cheer a stranger to these parts
We offer him dogberry wine.

   P'EI

Being fragrant, it is mistaken for the cinnamon or pepper tree;
With the bamboo its egg-shaped, pointed leaves blend best.
Though shone upon by the slanting afternoon sun,
The branches lie heavy and the trees look cold.

8) *Locust-tree Alley*
   WANG

A shady walk lined with locust-trees,
Under whose fallen leaves the green moss has spread!—
One of you page-boys at the gate there, sweep them up!
For any day now a monk from the temple may call.

   P'EI

Locust-tree Alley to the south of the gate
Is the route to Fair Lake;
The seasonal rains have descended on the mountains
And the leaves lie on the ground unswept.

9) *Lake Pavilion*

WANG

They have sent a boat to welcome you, my guest,
And lightly it moves across the lake.
Arrived at the pavilion, we shall now pledge each other
With the lotus flowers still in bloom all around us.

P'EI

Leaning on the balustrade, I see the waves in motion
And overhead a lone moon half lost in these mountains.
At the gorge the monkeys gibber and chatter,
Their cries wafted over the water by the breezes.

10) *South Knoll*

WANG

On an open boat we steer towards South Knoll—
North Knoll being further away by a whole stretch of water—
Straining our eyes, we scan every cottage on the shore
But seem to recognise nobody.

P'EI

On a lonely bark we drift with the wind and waves
By South Knoll near the lake's edge;
The sun drops to rest in its mountain cave,
And the waves seem suddenly to engulf us.

11) *Fair Lake*

WANG

I play on the flute as our boat nears the far shore
A plaintive tune of farewell at the close of day,
Then turn to the lake for a last look—
The white clouds are now curled round the green hills.

P'EI

Over the wide expanse of the water,
Sky and lake merge in one sparkling blue.
We moor the boat: we whistle loud and clear to the elements,
And the winds rise at our call.

12) *Willow Bank*

WANG

Laid out in rows and guarded by other trees,
These willows droop over their own clear images,
Unlike the sad willows along the Palace drains,
That weep the more as spring returns.

P'EI

The water is coloured green by their reflections;
Their branches fly in the breeze like gossamer threads;
Here at last they have their home
And need not pine for T'ao's 'Five Willows'.[1]

13) *Luan's Shoal*

WANG

The wind soughs and the current, swelled by the autumn rains,
Gurgles and splashes among the rocks,
Each fresh wave with its spray dashing upon another;
A hovering egret, its fears overcome, alights again on

the water.

P'EI

From the far bank we hear the din of the splashing;
We walk along the stream to the southern ford.
There the gulls and the ducks cross and re-cross the river,
And come close enough to mock us land-bound men.

14) *Gold Dust Fountain*

WANG

Drink daily of the Gold Dust Fountain
And expect to live to a thousand,
And be then escorted by a phoenix and a young dragon
Into the presence of the ruler of heaven.

P'EI

To that trickling fountain, sometimes flowing, sometimes dry,
With its gold and jade quite tangible,
At dawn, when one imbibes the purest essence of the air,
I shall go alone for that first, purest pail of spring water.

---

[1] T'ao Yüan-ming, who had five willow trees growing beside his
house, called himself 'Master of the Five Willows'; see *supra*.

15) *White Stone Shoal*
> WANG

White Stone Shoal, where the stream is clear
And the green rush grows thick,—
Where, if you live on either side of the river,
You will wash your silk by moonlight!

> P'EI

Treading gingerly on the white stones, I bend over the water
And dip my hands in the waves, listlessly.
At sundown, the river bank grows chilly
And the clouds themselves seem colourless.

16) *North Knoll*
> WANG

North Knoll lies north of the water
Where a balustrade shows through the trees;
A bay along the lake's southern shores
Is half hidden by the tree-tops of that wood.

> P'EI

Under North Knoll among these mountains
And overlooking Fair Lake, is where I would choose to dwell.
One day I would turn woodcutter,
Another day fill my boat with reeds and rushes.

17) *Bamboo Grove Pavilion*
> WANG

Seated alone in the bamboo grove,
I play on the guitar, then whistle with exhilaration

and abandon:

In the depth of these woods, imperceptibly
The moon floods its light all around me.

> P'EI

Even to approach Bamboo Grove Pavilion
Is to draw daily closer to the true way:
Only the birds fly in and out of here;
No mundane person trespasses on its seclusion.

18) *Magnolia Bank*
WANG

Like the lotus flower grown on a tree,
The pink magnolias sprinkle the hill-side;
Hidden in a gorge, unnoticed,
A thousand buds flower, then wither and die.

P'EI

The embankment is green with the spring grass,
A pleasing spot where men of fashion loiter,
Attracted, moreover, by the blossoming magnolias,
Which vie with the elegant lotus in shape and colour.

19) *Lacquer Garden*
WANG

That ancient sage[1] was no arrogant official
In cutting himself free from governmental affairs;
He was content with the station of a petty officer
Presiding over a few old varnish trees.

P'EI

From youth on, I have cared more for leisure than business;
Now I have fulfilled that self-exacted promise to retire.
In walking in this Lacquer Garden today,
We but follow in the wake of Chuang-tzu's tranquil ease.

20) *Pepper Garden*
WANG

Cinnamon wine is for the river goddess
And fragrant herbs for good and wise men,
But peppered broth offered on a clean mat
Is fare fit for the Lord of the Clouds himself.

P'EI

Its red thorns caught in your sleeve detain you;
Through its pungent aroma it then addresses you:
'As a condiment, pepper is beyond compare.
Pray, sir, take your pick of my fruit.'

---

[1] Chuang-tzu was an official in Ch'i-yüan ('Lacquer Garden'), where presumably at one time the varnish tree had flourished.

The Tower in P'ei Ti's House[1]

Sitting at ease within your town house,
You may gaze your fill of the cloud-capped mountains,
The setting sun below the flights of birds,
And the plains so calm in the stillness of autumn.

Thus secluded, you may see into that distant wood,
Being yourself unobserved under these eaves.
But, alas, many a visitor will call to look at the moon—
Let not your page-boy lock up too early!

To P'ei Ti[2]

Before this serene evening landscape,
I compose a few lines to speed you on your way.
Vacantly I gaze into the distance,
My chin resting against a *ju-i* stick.[3]
The plants wave in the breezes;
Scented orchids have sprouted along that fence.
From their sun-lit doorways
The farmers are coming forward to greet us.
Sweet spring has returned to the meadow,
And the pond is again glimmering with water.
Though the peach and plum blossoms are still to come,
Each branch of each tree is smothered with leaf and bud.
Hasten, then, my friend, to return—
Sowing time is not far off.

[1] c. 9, p. 155.   [2] c. 2, p. 27.
[3] *ju-i* stick: a curved ceremonial staff serving a variety of practical uses.

Addressed to P'ei Ti[1]

You have been absent,
Absent these many months.
Daily at the fountain
I recall how we walked hand in hand —
To walk hand in hand is to be of one mind —
And I sigh for your abrupt departure.
Thus I recall your presence,
And these lines reveal my deep devotion.

The Farm at 'Wang-ch'uan' after Soaking Rain[2]

They are starting a fire in the drenched woods after days
                                                of downpour,
To cook goosefoot and millet for men at work on the new land;
Over the silent flooded fields a white egret flaps its wings;
Among summer's shady branches a yellow oriole trills.

In pursuit of quiet, I watch the day-long hibiscus[3]
                                                in the mountains
And feed alone under the pines on the dewy mallow,
An old country fellow retired from the world's contests,
Somewhat hurt that the gulls should doubt his good intentions.

[1] c. 2, p. 13.
[2] c. 10, p. 187. The touchy old man whose guise Wang assumes in
this poem suggests the 750s as the date of composition.
[3] The hibiscus syriacus, whose blossoms last only a day.

Returning to 'Wang-ch'uan' in Spring[1]

I

At the sound of the temple bell from the gorge,
Fishermen and woodcutters disperse for their homes,
Leaving behind the hills in the calm evening light,
While I alone bend my steps towards the white clouds.

The spreading water-chestnut plant afloat on the pond,
The willow catkins blowing about in my face,
The soothing colour of the new grass on banks and slopes:
At my cottage door, I am loath to shut out spring.

II

For a year almost I was away from these mountains
And return now in time for the spring sowing.
In the rain the grass has dyed itself green;
Over the water the peach blossoms are a burning red.

A deformed mendicant friar most eloquent in preaching,
A hunchbacked elder, the sage of these hamlets—
With a coat thrown on and trailing my slippers, I rush out
to greet them,
And chat and laugh with these good neighbours before
my front door.

[1] Being originally two separate poems, the first entitled 'Returning to Wang-ch'uan' (c. 7, p. 123) and the second 'The Estate at Wang-ch'uan' (c. 10, p. 186). Returning after prolonged absence would seem to suggest that the poems belonged to the 750s rather than the early years at the estate.

Meng Hao-jan

○

Meng Hao-jan
(689–740)

Meng Hao-jan merits a place in this book in that his life was closely bound up with his surroundings in his native prefecture of Hsiang-yang. His name is often mentioned with that of Wang Wei, but Meng's talents were just not of the same order. T'ao and Hsieh, Wang Wei and Liu Tsung-yüan, though poles apart in disposition and outlook, were remarkable men who, with the confidence of unusual powers, gave something of themselves in their poems. Meng, in contrast, was a supremely accomplished craftsman who had little of real interest to reveal about his own being. In the collected works of each of the others there is an innate consistency; in Meng's one finds no more than some degree of similarity of theme and style. For the exterior of the man did not match his inner nature, and the reader who is attracted by the unworldly sentiments professed in one poem is likely to be repelled by the mundane desires expressed in another. Nevertheless, Meng's love for his native district was quite unfeigned, and in his Hsiang-yang poems he shakes off the affectation and self-pity that mar so many of his other poems.

If, however, the man lacked weight, the deficiency was amply compensated for by a great personal charm. Meng was tall and had a certain presence. During his year's stay in the capital Ch'ang-an, he dominated literary gatherings by improvising verses of exquisite phrasing, declaimed in a suitably compelling manner. Li Po, who was a younger contemporary, was fascinated even after over a dozen years' acquaintance:

I adore dear Master Meng,
Whose charm is known to all the world:

In his youth he renounced official honours;

In old age he reposes beneath the pines in the hills.[1]

And if even Li Po was captivated, the world at large readily succumbed to Meng's personal attractiveness.

But in the matter of the writing of verse Meng was in absolute earnest. Throughout a rather aimless life, his interest in poetry never abated. From an early age he worked day and night on his poems rather than at the classics that he and his younger brother Hsi-jan were taught, for the family, a respectable one with a learned tradition, owned a fair measure of land in the outskirts of Hsiang-yang (i.e., Siangyang in Hupeh Province), and the brothers were not obliged to aim at an official career. Hsiang-yang was a prefectural town with its own history and tradition, and even in his youth Meng played the role of local notable by helping the needy and relieving the distressed. Moreover, he had a gift for friendship and cultivated a wide circle of acquaintances. But when he was in the mood, he would repair to one of the temples or monasteries in the hills nearby and assume the guise of 'hermit'.

At the age of thirty-nine, Meng made a sudden bid for official rank by going to Ch'ang-an to take part in the examinations. By Chinese count, he was forty, at which age men like Wang Wei, having devoted half a lifetime to the civil service, thought of retiring to the hills. But in 728 Wang Wei was still young, and Meng and Wang became friends. (After Meng's death, Wang painted his portrait from memory.) Without seeking permission, Wang sometimes brought Meng into his own office in the Palace. On one such occasion the Emperor Hsüang-tsung entered unannounced and Meng hid under a couch. When the amused Emperor commanded Meng to present himself and recite some of his poems, Meng lost his usual aplomb and read out lines that failed to please. In particular, it was related, he chanted the line:

Being devoid of talent, I was rejected by my prince;[2]

to which the royal retort was: 'We are maligned. Rejected

[1] 'To Meng Hao-jan' in Wang Ch'i (ed.), *Li T'ai-po ch'üan-chi*, Ssu-pu pei-yao ed., c. 9, p. 1a.

[2] 'Returning to the hills at the end of the year', p. 69; Ssu-pu pei-yao ed., c. 3, p. 1b.

indeed! You who never sought our patronage!' Meng left
Ch'ang-an after a year's profitless stay. Less than a decade
later, in 737–8, when he had returned to Hsiang-yang, he
served briefly under Chang Chiu-ling, who had a nominal post
in Ching-chou (i.e., Kiangling also in Hupeh Province). For
a few months Meng was able to wear an official's hat and
robes, which probably cured him of further desire for office.

The visit to Ch'ang-an was preceded by a year of travel,
and followed probably by another four. It would be in the
spring of 727 that, at the Yellow Crane Tower in Wuchang
(in Hupeh Province), Li Po sped Meng on his way to Yang-
chow,[1] their acquaintance dating from Li's visit to Hsiang-
yang in the previous year.[2] Meng doubtless went sightseeing
along the route, especially when wind-bound. After staying
for some time in Yangchow (in Kiangsu Province), where
he made many friends, Meng went south into Chekiang,
visiting Kuei-chi and some of the river and hill scenery
celebrated by Hsieh Ling-yün on his way to Yung-chia in
422. Meng reached Ch'ang-an early in 728,[3] after battling
against the snow in the last stages of his journey, and early in
729 left Ch'ang-an for the other capital Loyang[4] (in Honan
Province). From Loyang, where he spent the spring and
probably the early part of summer, he took a boat and set out
once again for the 'hills and streams of Wu and Yüeh'[5] (i.e.,
Southern Kiangsu, and Chekiang), reaching the mouth of the
Chientang river near Hangchow in the eighth month, in time
to watch the autumn tidal bores.[6] He seems to have spent the
next three years in Chekiang,[7] visiting places he had already
known and venturing much farther. The Tientai Mountains

---

[1] 'Sending Meng Hao-jan off to Yangchow at the Yellow Crane
Tower', *Li T'ai-po ch'üan-chi*, c. 15, p. 15b.
[2] See Chan Ying, *Li Po shih-wen hsi-nien*, 1958, p. 5.
[3] See 'Meeting with snow on the way to the Capital', p. 118; Ssu-pu
pei-yao ed., c. 3, pp. 11a–b: and 'An Early Spring in Ch'ang-an',
p. 200; Ssu-pu pei-yao ed., c. 2, pp. 4b–5a.
[4] See 'Returning to the hills at the end of the year': and 'Convalescing
in the Lee Garden', p. 149; Ssu-pu pei-yao ed., c. 4, p. 6a.
[5] 'From Loyang to Yüeh', p. 112; Ssu-pu pei-yao ed., c. 3, p. 10a.
[6] 'Sailing on the Chientang', p. 206; Ssu-pu pei-yao ed., c. 4, p. 10a.
[7] See 'Lines addressed to Hsieh Nan-ch'ih and Assistant Magistrate
Ho of Kuei-chi after a long stay in Chekiang', p. 189; Ssu-pu pei-yao
ed., c. 2, p. 7b.

with their hermit and mythological associations were a favourite haunt, but he also visited Wenchow (i.e., Hsieh's Yung-chia) and made sea trips along the coast, so that he probably saw every noteworthy sight. And on his journey home up the Yangtze he had another good look at Lu-shan. Thus from this period of Meng's travels we have poems on Lu-shan, on Kuei-chi and the Fuchun river, on the Tientai Mountains and on Wenchow.

There were other trips, to Tungting Lake, to Szechuan and, probably in the winter of 737–8, again down the Yangtze to the coast.[1] For the purpose of this discussion, however, by the time of his return to Hsiang-yang in the summer of 732 or 733, he had seen all that he had set out to see. The Tientai Mountains were sanctified ground, but Kuei-chi, with its history and myths, its hills and numerous streams, its lush green valleys and luxuriant woods and groves, seemed to him the counterpart of Hsiang-yang. And it is with Kuei-chi that he makes comparison when he sings the praises of Hsiang-yang:

Hill for hill, stream for stream,

Hsiang-yang excels the vaunted Kuei-chi.

Whereas Meng knew Kuei-chi only as a visitor, his descriptions of the Hsiang-yang landscape were based on his complete knowledge of the area as a native; they contain such intimate details as a garden and bamboo grove shared by several families, or schoolboys reading aloud in a thatched cottage, or the boat changing course repeatedly to avoid the precipices and deep pools and its prow being turned right-about in the setting sun. Local pride and a real love of every watercourse and every hill and mound in the town's environs combine to infuse into these poems a spontaneity and naturalness that distinguish them from strings of lines of consummate skill.

Although he claimed all his life to be a recluse, Meng was one only in the sense that he lived outside the sphere of

---

[1] See 'A View of Lu-shan from Poyang Lake' (p. 11; Ssu-pu pei-yao ed., c. 1, p. 2ᵇ), in which he appears to be tied to a schedule while in active service at an overnight stop half way on his journey to the coast.

officialdom and that he was at liberty to abide in his own house
or wander where he would. He did, to be sure, seek the
instruction of Buddhist monks and Taoist priests; and he
repeatedly expressed his admiration for hermits of earlier
times such as P'ang Te-kung of Hsiang-yang. But no man was
more gregarious than Meng, who was fond of good company,
good food and good living. The bream, which abounds in the
region and is mentioned more than once in his poems, was his
favourite fish dish. He is reported to have spurned the offer of
an official post from the celebrated Han Ch'ao-tsung, who in
734 became Roving Commissioner of Provincial Affairs
stationed in Hsiang-yang, and whom Li Po sought out as a
prospective patron. Meng had just sat down to a sumptuous
meal and was in the midst of an animated discussion when
someone reminded him that he had an appointment with Han
that very day to travel together to the capital. Meng there-
upon declared that nothing would induce him to leave the
table at the beginning of a feast, and went on drinking. Han,
angry at the affront, withdrew his offer and set off by himself.
And Meng died of a malignant tumour seriously aggravated
by the fish and seafood he would not abstain from. But the
love of food and company was really part of the zest with
which he encountered new experiences and enjoyed the old
and familiar. The same zest characterised his seeking out new
places and new acquaintances. Indeed he was probably the
only one of the five poets represented in this book who some-
times went exploring by himself.

Hsiang-yang, a prefectural town in the T'ang as in later
dynasties, is situated on the south bank of the river Han (i.e.,
Hanshui), which, soon after passing the town in its eastward
flow, turns south to join the Yangtze at Wuhan. Hsiang-yang,
which lay on one of the main routes from the north to the
south, was of considerable commercial and strategic im-
portance. There was much river traffic, the Han being already
wide at this point. Facing Hsiang-yang on the north bank was
the town of Fancheng, administratively part of Hsiang-yang
prefecture. Ferry boats plied between Hsiang-yang and Fan-
cheng and other towns and villages on either bank. Meng does
not mention Fancheng, but Deer Gate Hill, where he spent

a period of his life and with which he is usually associated, is on the north bank, though fifteen kilometres south-east of Hsiang-yang. The 'solitary island' on the river is situated midway between Hsiang-yang and Deer Gate Hill, the title of the poem being derived from Hsieh Ling-yün, whose Solitary Island on the Yung-chia river Meng had visited and written about in a poem now lost.

Of the other hills mentioned by Meng, Hsien Hill, Wan Hill and Ch'u View Hill are all near Hsiang-yang; Fragrant Hill, over a hundred kilometres away in the Ta-hung Mountains, is in another prefecture. Besides the Han itself, there seemed to be a large number of streams and watercourses in and around Hsiang-yang. Meng was obviously a skilled oarsman, as at home on the waters of his native district as on dry land, and our selection ends with two short poems, one about the sails on the river Han, the other about Meng himself paddling a boat all over Hsiang-yang.

Meng's descriptive lines are sometimes strikingly apt, with an element of surprise contrived by the unusual syntax or the tension centred on a particular word in a line. The aptness and surprise are strengthened by the antithesis contained in the carefully balanced couplet. Thus Tu Fu, who was pre-eminent in the use of the same devices, pays a handsome tribute to Meng:

And I think, too, of Meng Hao-jan of Hsiang-yang,

Each one of whose pellucid verses enriches the memory.[1]

Apart from the arresting line and the pervasive rhetoric, the general impression conveyed by Meng's descriptions is one of superabundant colourfulness, which may indicate a greater concern with semblance than with the inward spirit. In his quest of hermits, and immortals, too, he seems more attracted by venerable appearance or quaint setting than by their transmitted gospel. Thus he describes in verse the Taoist friend to whom he addresses the poem written on the little island, Master White Cloud, at the very mention of whose name some poets would have fled:

[1] Ch'iu, *Tu Shao-ling chi hsiang-chu*, c. 17: Vol. VII, p. 82. For a translation of the whole stanza, see Tu Fu 'On the Writing of Verse' in Volume III of this series.

Being at leisure, he cultivates the divine purple fungus,
But has come to town today to buy medicinal herbs.
His hermitage is on Deer Gate Hill,
Where daily he listens to the rushing torrents.
Airily waving a fan of white feathers,
He treads measured paces in his straw sandals;
But the news of a summons to the Imperial court
Sends him flying to the stream to wash his ears.[1]

There is too much gaudiness and finery and calculated effect
here for any hermit. It seems typical also that Meng should
travel on horseback for a whole day in order to visit a monk
on a hill named 'Fragrant' and pervaded by a heavy scent.
However, if colourfulness seems a fault, Meng's keen aware-
ness of colour effects, for example, in 'A Visit to Deer Gate
Hill' and some of the other translated pieces, and in one of his
Lu-shan poems,[2] and indeed of sound effects, is certainly a
virtue.

It is in his portrayal of the Hsiang-yang scene that Meng
has added something new to Chinese poetry, for he has
succeeded, in spite of a certain propensity to formal description,
in demonstrating that a lively sketch of the local scene is of
greater interest than studied accounts of the wild and grand
and remote. His most accomplished lines and couplets have
undoubtedly made a certain impact on later writers, but the
real contribution of Meng consists in directing attention to
the intimate and familiar in the rural and suburban scene, to a
pretty, though not startlingly beautiful, landscape in which
ordinary folk, who are neither poets and artists nor farmers
and cowherds, live their rather commonplace lives.

Few of Meng's poems are dated, although the locality or
occasion is generally indicated in the title of each poem. The
itinerary of his travels above is reconstructed mainly from his
poems. In the selection here presented, the poems are arranged
according to subject matter to form a sequence on the theme
of Meng Hao-jan's Hsiang-yang.

For my translations I have used the text in Hsiao Chi-tsung

[1] 'Master White Cloud comes on a visit', p. 56; Ssu-pu pei-yao ed.,
c. 1, p. 12b.
[2] 'A View of Lu-shan from Poyang Lake'.

(ed.), *Meng Hao-jan shih shuo*, Commercial Press 1969, which is based on a collation of various earlier editions; references in the footnotes are to that edition. I have also inserted references to the Ssu-pu pei-yao edition of *Meng Hao-jan chi*.

Ch'u View Peak[1]

Hill for hill, stream for stream,
Hsiang-yang excels the vaunted Kuei-chi.
Highest among our hills is Ch'u View Peak,
Which until now I have not ascended.

Steep precipices that seem chiselled
Supporting a crown towering above all others —
On a clear day I venture to climb to the summit
And am greeted by a view of limitless expanse:

The lakes and marshes of Ch'u laid out like a map before me,
Perhaps even the Peach Blossom Ravine where the fisherman
                                        lost his way.
By dusk I descend to return on my horse
While through the creepers the moon shines on a deep stream.

A Visit to Deer Gate Hill[2]

I set out eagerly in the light of dawn,
Riding on the current to a far shore of rocky hills.
On the sands the waterfowl are barely distinguishable;
The trees in the distance look all alike.

[1] pp. 54–5; Ssu-pu pei-yao ed., c. 1, p. 12a. Ch'u View Hill, eight *li* to the south-west of Hsiang-yang, was named after the campaign in 301 B.C., in which the invading Ch'in army went up the hill to study the fortifications of a Ch'u town nearby. It later acquired the meaning of 'hill from which to survey the Ch'u state'; hence the boast in the line: The lakes and marshes of Ch'u laid out like a map before me.
[2] p. 14; Ssu-pu pei-yao ed., c. 1, pp. 2b–3a. Deer Gate Hill, thirty *li* south-east of Hsiang-yang, was where Meng Hao-jan settled some time after the writing of this poem. The hill was named after a Han dynasty temple, which had two sculptured deer at its entrance.

At length I approach Deer Gate Hill,
Its blue-green haze clearing in the bright morning.
The river winds round its several pools and precipices;
So near its destination, my boat repeatedly changes course.

I have heard of P'ang Te-kung of old,[1]
Who disappeared into this hill to gather herbs,
The golden torrent with whose waters he prepared his elixir
And the moss-covered stone slab that was his couch.

Being moved to wonder by accounts of this ancient worthy,
I clamber ashore impatient to trace his footsteps.
Localities and objects connected with him are indeed there:
That transcendent manner of his is now quite unknown.

When, then, did he vanish with the white clouds?
His cinnamon trees still are flourishing!
My curiosity remains not fully satisfied
As I turn my prow right-about in the evening sun.

Returning to Deer Gate Hill at Night[2]

From the temple on the mound a bell tolls at dusk;
At Fishermen's Ferry Bridge the noisy crowd waits to
                                              cross the river.

As others are borne to villages along the sandy banks,
So I too take a boat to return to Deer Gate Hill.

Over Deer Gate the moon is shining through the mists
                                              and the trees

And I find myself standing before P'ang's old hermitage,[3]
The precipice that was his gate and the pines that marked
                                              his path,

Long since forsaken by all but the chance visitor.

---

[1] P'ang Te-kung, celebrated hermit of Hsiang-yang towards the end
of the Later Han. He spent the earliest part of his life in the vicinity
of Hsien Hill and then, early in the third century, became a complete
recluse on Deer Gate Hill.
[2] p. 59; Ssu-pu pei-yao ed., c. 2, p. 1a.
[3] See note to previous poem.

The Pool below Wan Hill[1]

Perched on a rock, I bait my hook:
The water is transparent, my mind unclouded.
The fish weave in and out of the reflected trees;
The monkeys swing from the vine on the island.

Two goddesses divested themselves of their ornaments
As a gift to the lucky Chiao-fu on this hill;[2]
No such inspired adventures befall me
As, with my oar and a song, I row back under the moon.

To Chang Fifth on ascending Wan Hill on a day in autumn[3]

Wrapped up in white clouds on this northern hill,[4]
The recluse delights in his own enclosed world.
Others who climb the heights for the view
Find their mundane thoughts dismissed by each passing bird.

A tinge of sadness spread by the approaching twilight
Tempers the zest wakened by the brisk air of autumn,
As I watch the villagers hurrying towards their homes
Or patiently waiting on the sands for the ferry-boat.

Near the horizon the trees seem rows of cabbage;
On the darkening river the island floats like the

                                    crescent moon—
Another autumn we shall ascend a hill together
And celebrate over a jar of wine the Double Ninth.[5]

[1] p. 76; Ssu-pu pei-yao ed., c. 1, p. 10b.
[2] The legend of Cheng Chiao-fu and the goddesses who handed him their ornaments, which disappeared when he felt for them again in his pocket, is part of the local tradition of Hsiang-yang. Wan Hill is ten *li* west of Hsiang-yang.
[3] p. 22; Ssu-pu pei-yao ed., c. 1, p. 4a.
[4] Although situated to the west of Hsiang-yang, Wan Hill is referred to as the northern hill, being probably the northernmost of the Hsiang-yang hills on the south bank of the Han river.
[5] Festival falling on the ninth day of the ninth month, on which it was customary to go up a hill or high tower.

To Master White Cloud during a short stop at a solitary island on the river Han[1]

Tranquil flows the current of the Han:
When the water is low, the island appears,
And a deep pool on it hidden by the rocks,
And thick clusters of thin green bamboos near the shore.
No merman nor mermaid inhabits the sands,
But the timeless figure of a fisherman singing to himself.

I recall the time of your departure—
It seems but yesterday when we had the send off on the boat:
The sunset had given way to a glorious afterglow;
Among those present, some were cheerful, others dejected. —
Southwards I see Deer Gate Hill,
Which I now head for, homeward-bound but feeling lost.

Visiting Hsin O among the western hills[2]

Being afloat on the river in my boat,
I set out to visit my friend Hsin O.
At sunset on a fine day along this stream
One's eyes are diverted from the fish to the landscape:

Stones at the bottom of a clear pool,
The sandy shore along which the river meanders,
A fisherman among the bamboos on an island,
Schoolboys reading aloud in a thatched cottage.

Absorbed in talk, we let the evening slip by,
Our spirits heightened by autumn's first breezes;
For, though his fare be meagre,
My friend is wise and the best of company.

---

[1] p. 24; Ssu-pu pei-yao ed., c. 1, p. 4ᵇ. Wang Chiung, who lived for some time at Deer Gate Hill, styled himself Master White Cloud; see Introduction.
[2] p. 162; Ssu-pu pei-yao ed., c. 2, p. 2ᵃ.

Going by boat to the water pavilion of
Ch'en Eldest on a summer evening[1]

For a breath of cool air, repair to the water pavilion:
By evening I ply my oar and hasten there.
The stream mirrors the bamboos and pines along its banks;
I reach the pool and smell the fragrant lotus.

A lad of the hills performs a dance in the kiosk,
The birds chiming in with his half tipsy song.
I have scarce begun to take in the scene,
When night falls and leaves me with the cool I sought.

Lines addressed to Hsin Eldest from South Pavilion
on a night in summer[2]

Twilight fades suddenly when the sun drops below the hill;
Silently the moon rises over the pond.
With my hair loosened, I enjoy the cool of evening,
Reclining in this pavilion with its windows thrown open.
The lotus flowers send out their sweet fragrance;
The dew from the bamboo leaves drips audibly on the water.
I wished to fetch my guitar —
But I have no one to play to!
Thus my thoughts have turned to you, my friend,
And I lie awake at night wondering how you are.

Visiting the two gentlemen Wu and Chang at their
country home by Sandalwood Stream after the winter solstice[3]

What a natural setting for one's country dwelling
On the near side of Sandalwood Stream!
The adjoining villas of two friends
And a bamboo grove shared by several families
On a site directly facing South Hill,
Chosen for its view, not for its seclusion.

---

[1] p. 89; Ssu-pu pei-yao ed., c. 3, p. 4b, with the title 'Going by boat to the villa of T'eng, the recluse, on a summer evening'.
[2] p. 43; Ssu-pu pei-yao ed., c. 1, pp. 9a-b.
[3] p. 163; Ssu-pu pei-yao ed., c. 2, p. 2a, contains, after l. 6, four additional cliché-ridden lines that do not add to the interest of the poem.

To laze and sun oneself in the courtyard
Or paddle with an oar on the water
Or, detached from the world's affairs,
Drift mid stream according to the heart's desire,
Idling away the time fishing without a catch,
Or set out with a punt-pole to look up some old acquaintance!

I, who claim also to live a hermit's life,
Am mildly surprised by their carefree mode of existence
With the plum blossoms that burst upon the closing year
And the half-green willows promising an early spring;
Only the birds are missing, flown south with the wild geese,
And the bream with its high-arched back still stays hidden.

Laying down my cup, I ask: 'Did ever guest enjoy
                                    himself more
Since the drunk Governor Shan's visits to the
                                 Hsi's garden pond?'[1]

Waiting for Ting Eldest at the mountain hut of Master Lai-kung[2]

The westering sun passes beyond the hills;
Darkness creeps over each ravine and gully.
The moon above the pines sends a chill through the night;
In the breeze the fountain hums a jolly tune.

The woodcutters have long left the woods;
The tardiest bird is back on its perch;
You, my friend, have kept me waiting in vain
Alone with my guitar among the creepers by the path.

[1] Shan Chien (253–312), while stationed in Hsiang-yang as Military Governor of the region, frequented the house of the Hsi family and spent much of his time near their garden pond. The perpetually drunk Governor Shan is part of the local tradition.
[2] pp. 9–10; Ssu-pu pei-yao ed., c. 1, p. 2a.

Visiting Master Chan on Fragrant Hill[1]

I start in the morning on my ride
To a hill far beyond the distant haze,
Covering a hundred *li* of mountainous terrain
Until at sunset I reach the famous hill.

At the mouth of a ravine I hear a temple bell,
And a distinctive fragrance permeates the woods.
With a stick I find my way up the slope,
Leading my unsaddled horse towards the monastery.

A stone gateway divides light from the shade within;
A bamboo-lined path guides me through a maze of trees.
My Buddhist friend so rejoices at my coming,
We converse all night long, not stopping even at dawn.

All my life I have sought after the true recluse —
I would wander for days in search of some wondrous sight.
Before me now — an ancient hermit who emerged with the
                                        morning clouds,
The monks returning from the hills for their evening prayers,

A melodious cascading stream beneath the pines,
And moss on cliffs like patina on old bronzes.
I would willingly remain on this hill,
Renouncing both my fleshly self and the world!

---

[1] p. 1; Ssu-pu pei-yao ed., c. 1, p. 1a. Fragrant Hill, eighty *li* north
of the town of Kingshan, would be part of the Ta-hung Shan range,
situated to the south-east of Hsiang-yang itself as well as Deer Gate
Hill. From Deer Gate Hill, the distance to Fragrant Hill would be
under 100 kilometres (200 *li*), much of the route being along the Ta-
hung Shan range.

To Chang Han from the pavilion on Hsien Hill
overlooking the river Han[1]

At windy Hsien Head the current is swift;
The full sails are like flapping wings.
I lean against the railing and ask:
'Will Chang Han be among those coming this way?'

Boating on North Stream[2]

North Stream is high in all weathers;
Paddling with an oar brings the whole of

Hsiang-yang within reach.
Whether ploughing upstream or gliding downstream,
There is more good sport than on the Five Great Lakes.

[1] pp. 210–11; Ssu-pu pei-yao ed., c. 4, p. 10b.
[2] p. 210; Ssu-pu pei-yao ed., c. 4, p. 11a.

Liu Tsung-yüan

o

Liu Tsung-yüan
(773–819)

Liu Tsung-yüan was that rare phenomenon among traditional Chinese writers, a belletrist who was also in the fullest sense an intellectual. Without being a philosopher or a dedicated scholar, he had an enquiring mind ready to question every assumption and examine every subject with a candour far exceeding that of most philosophers and scholars. And his critical attitude was exceptional among literary men. In the sphere of literature, Liu was the creator of a plain style in descriptive and narrative prose and a gifted, though selective, writer of verse.[1] In particular, he wrote on landscape, a subject which he probably only took up because he was compelled to spend fourteen years in remote parts of the T'ang empire, ten of them in what was then a wilderness, another four in what amounted to a clearing in a jungle.

For successive generations Liu's family, who were originally from P'u-chou (i.e., Yungtsi in Shansi Province), had been officials, sometimes in distinguished positions; but the main influences in his life were those of his father, a forthright man with a strong sense of justice, who served chiefly in the capital, and of his mother, a highly educated woman from a similar official background, who taught him his books as a child. It was in their house in the western suburbs of Ch'ang-an that Liu was born. At the age of eleven, Liu, who had sisters but no brother, accompanied his father to a post in the Wuhan area (in Hupeh Province); from there, they went on a visit to T'an-chou (i.e., Changsha in Hunan Province) and probably also to other places in that part of the Yangtze basin. (The short period he spent in Wuhan is referred to in one of

---

[1] See also Ssu-k'ung T'u, 'A Colophon to the Collected Poems by Liu Tsung-yüan' in Volume III of this series.

his Yung-chou poems.) In 788 his father was made an Assistant Censor and took part in the review of a judicial case in the teeth of determined opposition from a powerful clique at court. The verdict was reversed, but Censor Liu found himself banished to K'uei-chou (i.e., Fengkieh in Szechuan Province) in the following year. Young Liu, who was then sixteen, was already busy with preparations for the examinations, so that he remained in the capital with his mother. Three years later, in 792, his father was cleared and reinstated at court. The incident and the example of his father left an indelible mark on Liu.

In 793 Liu passed his metropolitan examination, at which a successful fellow candidate was Liu Yü-hsi, who was a year older than Liu and who became a staunch friend. In the same year, Liu's father died. In 796, at the age of twenty-three, Liu was appointed to his first post as Collator of Books in the Imperial Archives, in which capacity he wrote various commemorative essays, two of them about shrines at which the Emperor prayed for rain. In 798 he passed the Great Literary Scholarship Examination and was made Palaeographer. His talents having become known, Liu was much sought after as a writer of congratulatory addresses and similar compositions, so that he was kept near the capital in his next post as Assistant Magistrate of Lantien (near which Wang Wei's estate had been situated), which he held from 801 to 803.

Liu's political career began with his appointment in 803 as an Assistant Censor; Han Yü, with whom Liu's name was later to be coupled, was an immediate colleague. Liu was now thirty and already had firm convictions on questions of government and administration. As a member of the Censorate, he was at the centre of affairs and came into frequent contact with others holding similar liberal views, which included his friend Liu Yü-hsi. Liu's opportunity came early in 805 with the accession of Shun-tsung, who, being an invalid, handed over the reins of government to Wang Shu-wen, who had been tutor to the Emperor while still Crown Prince. Wang, who had held strongly reformist views with which Shun-tsung had concurred, had led a small liberal faction at court, to which both Liu and Liu Yü-hsi had been drawn. After his precipitate rise to power, Wang proceeded to instal those who were of his faction, or whom he trusted, in key positions. Both Liu and Liu Yü-hsi were given posts, Liu as Assistant Secretary in the Board of Rites. Certain measures, long overdue and immediately popular, were adopted in the first instance: dismissal of a number of corrupt officials, abolition of certain inordinate privileges of the eunuchs and palace servants, a partial disbanding of the palace serving-women, abolition of non-statutory taxes, annulment of all taxes in arrears, the recalling of able and upright officials unjustly banished. The policies and long-term measures of the reformists were still in a stage of deliberation.

The enterprise turned on the person of the Emperor, who had delegated his authority to Wang Shu-wen. The Ministers who had previously been in power now joined with the army commanders and the eunuchs in a palace revolution, in which Shun-tsung was forced to abdicate in favour of the crown prince, who became the Emperor Hsien-tsung. Wang Shu-wen and his friends were all together but a dozen or so men, with no other ally than the deposed sovereign. They were summarily banished to remote prefectures in several directions. Liu had been in office but a few months. He had probably cherished grand designs for the State; he now had the prospect of an uncomfortable journey lasting a month or more to Shao-chou (i.e., Paoking in Hunan Province). His friend Liu Yü-hsi was banished to Lang-chou (i.e., Changteh, also in Hunan). And even before Liu had reached his destination, he was further banished to Yung-chou (i.e., Lingling, also in Hunan), a prefecture yet further south by over a hundred kilometres, where he would be Marshal.

Liu reached Yung-chou in the winter of 805 and, having nowhere to live, stayed at Lung-hsing Temple, situated on a hill overlooking the Hsiang river. He was accompanied by his mother and two male cousins, one of them the faithful Tsung-chih, who appears in 'The Shrine in a Stone Pagoda in Fa-hua Temple'. (Liu had married in the year of his first official appointment, but his wife had died three years later.) Although he occupied an official post, he had no assigned duties and, being somewhat lost in that strange and outlandish place, found consolation in surveying the surrounding scenery from the hill itself and from the temple's towers. A mud wall blocked the view from the family's rooms, which faced north and were rather dark. As Marshal Extraordinary, he had no administrative power, but the local people and the monks were under his command, and he derived undisguised satisfaction from issuing his first order, that a second gate be opened up on the west side of the temple wall and a little porch erected beside it, to enable him to see the trees in the valley and the Hsiang river flowing past. It seemed to him one deed accomplished and, therefore, to be recorded. The record was the first of a whole series of essays, on the local temples, on the scenery, on pavilions and gardens.

Yung-chou was sparsely populated by a mixture of tribesmen and Chinese farmers. Lingling itself, the county town, which was also the seat of the prefecture, had been fortunate in its magistrate at about the time of Liu's arrival. The countryside was deserted but peaceful, and the low prices, to someone fresh from Ch'ang-an, quite unheard of. Liu drew a salary for which he had no use. His frustrated political ambition found scope in an imaginary reign over the hills and valleys in which few showed the slightest interest. Furthermore, it conferred on one a real sense of power to be able to purchase on the spot a hill that caught one's fancy for what one would have spent on a few rolls of the Classics in the capital. Labour, too, was cheap when not actually under his command, and from the hills came a ready supply of timber and bamboo. Gradually, then, when he had abandoned hope of an early recall and came to feel more settled, Liu began exploring and mentally colonising whole stretches of the wilderness, giving new names to hillocks and streams and claiming each discovery as a conquest. From this poetical subjugation he proceeded to make actual alterations to the contours of hill and slope, mound and hollow, and, when he had no right to do so, was prepared to acquire ownership in order to suit the terrain to the type of view deemed by him as appropriate to it. Each such occasion was carefully recorded, and that a stonemason stood by to have the account written in the Marshal's own hand transferred and carved on a stone tablet was an added incentive. In the process, Liu founded a new colony for Chinese literature, the landscape essay.

Liu's stay in Yung-chou lasted nearly ten years, during which he gathered a small literary circle around him. He generally found the Prefect congenial, but prefects came and went. Students from distant parts in the south, however, travelled to Yung-chou to seek his advice; and in giving them instruction in person, as well as by correspondence, Liu formulated his own ideas on scholastic questions and especially on the art of prose, in the writing of which he achieved a pre-eminence shared by only one other of his contemporaries. For his province was not limited to landscape but comprised all manner of subjects. The other outstanding prose-writer was his former colleague Han Yü,[1] who was older than Liu by five years and who remained a friend in spite of their political differences and Liu's misfortunes. Han and Liu each had their own following. Han, later to become Principal of the Imperial Academy, headed a whole school of essayists. The number of Liu's followers was necessarily small, but their attainment was not the less, for they had the benefit of his personal instruction. The generosity shown by each of the two friends in commending the other's essays to his own pupils is indeed cheering. Han's prime quality was eloquence, and his prose was rhetorical and argumentative. Liu's was a meditative style, altogether denser, more closely reasoned and carrying greater substance. That in his isolation Liu found means to nourish his own mind and fulfil his early promise was at least in part due to his concern for the young scholars who sought his guidance and the stimulation of his correspondence with Liu Yü-hsi and Han Yü.

Early in 815, Liu, along with others who had been banished at the same time as himself, was suddenly recalled to the capital. Poems written on the journey up express hope and rejoicing tempered with gloomy foreboding. There was, in fact, no intention of keeping him in the capital, and a month after his return to Ch'ang-an, Liu was sent to Liu-chou (i.e., Liuchow in Kwangsi Province), to be Prefect over a region

---

[1] For some autobiographical essays by Han Yü, see Volume v of this series.

of jungle inhabited by tribesmen. Liu Yü-hsi was similarly re-banished, to Lien-chou (i.e., Linhsien in Kwangtung Pro-vince), and the two friends accompanied each other as far as Hengyang (about 125 kilometres north-east of Yung-chou). Liu's mother had died in Yung-chou, and he had with him only Tsung-chih and another male cousin. After fully three months of travelling, they reached Liu-chou, which had a sub-tropical climate that did not agree with them; twenty days after their arrival, Tsung-chih was taken ill and died.

Liu-chou, which bore his surname, presented a challenge to Liu, who was still eager to govern: the local customs were barbarous, theft and robbery rife, the town walls in disrepair, the water supply uncertain. Liu exerted himself to bring order and civilisation to the tribesmen. Wells were dug, the streets cleaned, the town walls repaired, a Confucian temple built and schools set up, slavery and other customs reformed. In the midst of these enlightening and beneficent activities, Liu also found occasion for essays and poems; he even took the time to build a pavilion. In 818, three years after his arrival, Liu's health began to fail. In the following year, an amnesty was proclaimed, but, when the courier sent to summon Liu reached Liu-chou, Liu Tsung-yüan was already dead.

Liu named as his literary executor Liu Yü-hsi, who, like Liu himself, had suffered two prolonged banishments on account of a fit of youthful enthusiasm and political zeal; thus Liu Yü-hsi edited Liu's collected works. In Liu-chou the tribesmen, who revered Liu like a god, erected a temple to his memory. But, for students of Chinese, Liu Tsung-yüan will always be associated with Yung-chou, where he did not govern but reigned over a desolate wilderness that is now part of the literary heritage.

Liu's interest in landscape was part of a deep-seated cosmic consciousness: landscape, though sympathetic and consoling, was only the surface of a hidden reality, to which he responded with a fervour not short of religious. Thus the hills were the bulgings of the earth's veins. And the heavens contained even greater mysteries, in the revolving sun and moon and stars, in the floating and dissolving clouds, in the atmosphere, and in the empyrean itself. The universe itself was a living organism, whose forces, as manifested in the storm or the growth and decay of vegetation or even in some jutting peak, were cause for wonder and repaid investigation. Thus Liu gives as one reason for his building of the pavilion by Fa-hua Temple: 'to watch the scenery in wind and rain, and study the elemental forces, and be uplifted to the highest stratum of the all-embracing atmosphere'. One could wish that Liu had had an opportunity of describing T'ai-shan or one of the other Holy Mountains, or the vast ocean; he would almost certainly have risen to the occasion.

But the hills, rivers, mounds and pools of Yung-chou were within easy reach, and they became part of his idiom. His moods coloured the landscape, which in turn gave shape to his feelings. Thus 'The Shrine in a Stone Pagoda in Fa-hua Temple' is an account of a pilgrimage, a deliberate search for the things he had come to associate with the sight of the temple on the hill in the distance: height and aspiration; a widened horizon and outlook; truth through revelation. He set out with all his faculties alerted, 'receptive to every delightful sensation', finding even the touch of the plants and leaves blandishing. And the landscape, too, seemed exuberant, sensuous and vital:

Charmed by a stream shaded by ever deepening pine woods,
We clambered up a passage hewn out of the rock's surface.
Layers of creeping plants trailed over the temple's roofs,
And the votive tablet was overspread with moss.

But his own turbulence of spirit—for he was in a serious dilemma, intellectually and morally—was embodied also in the starkness of the hill and the violence with which it seemed to erupt from the earth:

Two tall thickets stood their ground in mutual defiance
Over a sheer precipice with its flanks exposed—
A stupendous rock sticking out of the luxuriant vegetation,
Its tufty top overhanging river and lake.

It appears as if the earth's veins had erupted
Or a pillar fallen out of heaven—

Liu, who was fundamentally Confucian, shows in this poem Buddhist leanings, openly declaring that his hope 'rests in those offering a new way'. Because of its very contradictions, the poem is a remarkable piece of autobiography, a human document in which the man's intellectual fervour, his metaphysical urge and his religious bent are all clearly mirrored. For it is seldom indeed that we get a portrait of the whole man from a single poem or even an entire corpus of poems by a Chinese writer. Invariably social and literary conventions intervene, to screen, refract and dilute, until the resulting image is the pale shadow of a human figure. This poem is an honourable exception.

The dilemma remained, but Liu gradually acquired a calmer and more detached view of his surroundings. He had discovered that he could alter his mental existence by re-shaping the physical landscape, as, for example, in his poem 'Building West Pavilion by Fa-hua Temple':

I ordered servants to fell shrub and tree and undergrowth,
And erect a pavilion, arresting the slope of the mountain.
From chaos emerges order, a clean cut
                          removing earth's excrescences:
My pavilion soars and I float with the clouds.

Indeed when we read the other poems and essays about Fa-hua Temple, we wonder if it was the temple on the same hill up which he and his cousin had climbed with their 'backs bent and feet hobbling'. The 'Preface to the Poems written in West Pavilion' states briefly: 'Though situated at a considerable height, the temple was not inaccessible'. And on a visit at night, Liu describes the temple and pavilion as:

Vaulted by the galaxies of the night sky,
Safe and serene above the clouds and rainstorms.

In 'Ascending West Pavilion by night', from which the two lines are taken, and in 'Returning at night after an excursion to South Pavilion' (only the first half of which is here translated) the correlation between the landscape and the inner world is less close, for they have, as their theme, political exile as well as an excursion. Although there is much brooding, Liu's spontaneous delight in the natural scene remains unaffected: the pervasive influence of Hsieh is now and then held in check by a spirit of unconcern derived from T'ao. The two poems also tell us something about the manner in which

these excursions were undertaken; in 'Ascending West
Pavilion' even the presence of a guide is acknowledged.

Of the essays included in this selection, 'The Three Pavilions
of Lingling' (about 807) marks the beginning of Liu's active
interest in landscape gardening, which he was much concerned
to justify. The other essays also deal with attempts at land-
scape gardening by Liu himself and others. The essay on Ma-
t'ui Mountain is included for the sake of Liu's comments
rather than his description, which seems to have been based on
the account he had received from his relative. Liu's best
exposition of his ideas on beauty in landscape is to be found
in 'The Eastern Mound by Lung-hsing Temple', in which the
distinction he draws between the 'open' and 'confined' views
seems valid for all landscapes and gardens.

For my translations I have used *Liu Ho-tung chi*, Chung-
hua 1961 (being third impression of edition of 1960), and the
chüan and page references in the footnotes are to that edition.
(The *chüan* references are the same for the Ssu-pu pei-yao
edition of Chiang Chih-ch'iao's *Liu Ho-tung chi*.)

The Shrine in a Stone Pagoda in Fa-hua Temple[1]

Being sentimental and often in fits of melancholy,
To give scope to my aspirations in the bracing heights,
I cherished a plan of visiting the famous temple
On a peak to the east to which I look up daily.

We were gladdened by the sunshine after the rainstorm
And especially the sight of the trees and new grass.
For companion I had my devoted young cousin;[2]
Brushing against plants and leaves, we were receptive
                       to every delightful sensation.

[1] c. 43, pp. 710–11.
[2] His devoted cousin Tsung-chih, who followed him to Yung-chou in
805 and, subsequently, in 815 to Liu-chou; a man of considerable
learning who seems to have forgone all thoughts of a career of his
own.

Charmed by a stream shaded by ever deepening pine woods,
We clambered up a passage hewn out of the rock's surface.
Layers of creeping plants trailed over the temple's roofs,
And the votive tablet was overspread with moss.

Two tall thickets stood their ground in mutual defiance
Over a sheer precipice with its flanks exposed—
A stupendous rock sticking out of the luxuriant vegetation,
Its tufty top overhanging river and lake.

It appears as if the earth's veins had erupted
Or a pillar fallen out of heaven—
This primitive structure towers above a circle of cliffs,
Overshadowing a myriad objects all around.

A kalpa is no more than an instant,
A world no greater than the palm of one's hand:
To realise the emptiness of form harks back to a primal state;
To study sense-perception leaves petty thoughts behind.

Plagued by midges and buzzing insects—backs bent,
                                        feet hobbling,
After a climb that would have tired even the
                                mountain spirits—
Why all the effort to make our way up?
It's not for an ell of good that we diverge an inch.

In search of the unusual as far as the eye would reach,
Straining the ear to hear each harmonious sound—
The meaning of this I grasped that moment
And my mind was awakened as never before.

If the quest for the unknown should be discontinued,
The vital spark of tradition, too, would be quenched.
My hope rests in those offering a new way;
I have no use for 'the nominal' or 'the real'.

For to excel requires some external incentive
But to remain meekly silent is a sign of the light within.
To judge by your old-world manners, cousin,
You are undeniably of our clan:

Hiding yourself, renouncing fame and career,
Disdainfully rejecting the dust of this world,
Determined to exert yourself on my behalf,
Following my steps even when they tend in
                                        no certain direction.

By the temple we lingered till the close of day,
Gazing wistfully upon the distant fields and valleys,
The wild geese in a line in the setting sun,
The changing clouds like billowing waves.

What a variety of scenery we had reaped!
For the return journey, a long road ahead!
Like a stray log weary of further drifting
Or a drooping flag in some deserted fairground,

Even as men of old lamented when deflected from their aims,
So I find myself unable to act as I would.
But why be anxious about one's destiny?
There is a picture of Buddha in that pagoda,

Led up to by a secluded path a foot in width,
Enshrined in a bare room ten feet square:
His holy words will enlarge our heritage—
Before it let me daily make obeisance.

Returning at night after an excursion to South Pavilion[1]
(808)

In my heart I cherished always the hills and ravines;[2]
To roam among them was my natural inclination.
Mid way through life I was enticed into the civil service,
And busied myself in vain with divination and sacrifices.

Outwardly I conformed, following the beaten track;
Inwardly my admiration was for a few chosen vessels.
In my career, I was no born statesman;
Were I retired, I could not be a village hero.

Heaven had in store for me another fate,
And when the spirits decreed, there was no escape.
A sudden reverse of fortune brought me to grief!
I merited forsooth the sad disaster that befell me.

For the gods were indeed almighty
And my accusers were vociferous;
So I was plunged into this unending landscape,
Where I gave vent to my feelings by reciting *Li sao*.

I remembered from former years an appointment with the hills,
Which to keep, I set out vacantly in a skiff
Past my uncluttered office[3] backed by the slopes,
And my front window facing on the river's bank.

Through a succession of sinuous banks and reaches
And of cliffs and rocks I glided along,
And an islet—a mass of floating vegetation—
Which I mistook at first for a giant turtle,

Then past dense woods which broke the force of the wind
And pebbles which motionless checked the splashing waves.
The skies cleared to define a widened range of vision:
Woodcutters and hay-gatherers calling to one another,

[1] c. 43, pp. 715–17.
[2] The line echoes the opening lines of Hsieh Ling-yün's 'Reading in My Study' (p. 46 *supra*): 'Amidst the magnificent splendour of the capital / I still cherished the lonely hills and ravines.'
[3] 'uncluttered office': 'Uncluttered' or 'empty office' was Hsieh Ling-yün's phrase; see 'Reading in My Study' (p. 46, *supra*).

White gulls bobbing on the surface of the deep pool,
Yellow monkeys leaping from rock to rock up the precipice,
The belling deer at pasture as in the Ode,
The blissful fish under the bridge in the parable.

While lamenting that I should contemplate this scene alone,[1]
I would not deny myself a moment of good cheer.
As leaning over the carved railing I pondered,
I filled up my pitcher with unstrained wine.

My chaps busily crunching water-chestnuts,
My outstretched hand settling on a crab's claw,
I watched the pot simmering over a fire made with rice-stalks
To the sound of freshly caught fish being chopped up,

And vegetables from the fields taken out of baskets
Mixed with water-plants to lend flavour to the broth.
I called to mind Ch'ü Yüan's old fisherman
And the song he sang as he drank up the dregs.

I thought, too, of the ascetic Ch'en Chung-tzu,
Who revived himself by swallowing a worm-eaten plum.
Such austerity is utterly beyond me—
Though sunk in misery, I was content with my
                       hidden mode of existence,

With the snow-geese screaming on an island at the bend,
Over which the fragrant orchid spread its leaves,
And the western peaks reflecting the glow of evening,
And the waters of the Hsiao relentlessly flowing northward.

Dusk overtook us as we lingered;
Lights in the distance pin-pointed boats in convoy;
On the bare hills, leafless trees stood silent;
Under the autumnal moon the river broadened into an
                       expanse of light.

---

[1] Another echo of Hsieh Ling-yün's poems generally, though not of any particular one represented in this book; see Chapter on Hsieh, *supra*.

Here is a lesson I would pass on to my disciples—
To attain consummate skill, have regard to what you wield:
In the shallows shun the long oar
And in deep waters put away the punting pole.

Led on by the moonlit prospect, I seized the boatman's paddle;
I broke into a plaintive song and wildly tapped the boards.
The skiff glided in mid stream, flattering my wayward impulse,
And I felt myself to be borne on wings.

We moored, having reached our stopping place.
The winds across the valley soughed;
The rushing torrent sent all flying before it;
Along the deserted path hungry beasts were growling.

[The second half of the poem contains the poet's lament of his
own lot, his reflections on recent events in the Empire—
which supply clues to the date of the poem—and his hope of
being recalled so as to return to the simple pleasures of country
life in his old home in the suburbs of the capital.]

Ascending West Pavilion by night
after a visit to Ch'ao-yang Cliff[1]

To be banished is not to choose the life of a recluse,
Nor a ramble among the hills a distant excursion:
It is anger that gnaws at my heart;
I lay no claim to the true title of hermit.

Descending from the cliff where I traced the course
                                         of the river,

Passing dark caverns that conceal scaly dragons,
Suddenly I see the open valley spread out before us
Overhung by the tree-tops of thick, dark woods,

And on the peak itself West Pavilion,
Backed by the roofs and columns of the temple,
Vaulted by the galaxies of the night sky,
Safe and serene above the clouds and rainstorms.

[1] c. 43, pp. 711–12.

A pity this is not my native district
And that I lend no lustre to the local produce!
For though in my boyhood I visited the Yangtze valley,
For generations we were officials in the areas

around the capital.

Our old villa is by the banks of the river Feng,[1]
Where we have our fields, part fertile, part barren,
And our summer-houses and terraces up on a mound,
And a pond formed by combining several hollows.

But I was afire with worldly ambition
And, not without scruples, left my voluntary seclusion.
This feeble frame proved indeed quite ineffectual:
My mean abilities were frittered away in vexatious trivialities.

I am resigned to leading the life of a prisoner;
My deep shame I have tried to live down.
My courtyard is a hotbed of weeds and mugwort;
The cracks in my window are sealed by cobwebs.

In my ramblings I am guided by a dweller of these hills,
Who with his long pole propels a light sampan.
We drink of the river water, purer than the best distillation;
For viands we have the herbs and fruit of the land.

As has been said by those who attained the way—
Merrymaking consists not in pipes and strings;
Through carefree wandering dismiss abstruse doctrine;
In plain living find refuge from clamour and hubbub.

The clarion cock reminds us we have travelled all night;
Through the sounds of wind and rain we hear its

cock-a-doodle-doo.

As I leave the boat, I cry out: 'Friend, some other livelong day
I will help with the cooking on our expedition.'

---

[1] The villa was in the western suburbs of Ch'ang-an.

Building West Pavilion by Fa-hua Temple[1] (809)

Banished to Ch'u's southern extreme,
I roam an unending world of hills and streams.
I climbed up to the highest temple in the district,
Wandering as always with zest and abandon.

The mountain's west face was a sheer drop,
Where an immortal could peep at the world of men.
How strange! There I found myself as in a ravine,
Eyes, hands, feet alike obstructed by thorns and brushwood.

I ordered servants to fell shrub and tree and undergrowth,
And erect a pavilion, arresting the slope of the mountain.
From chaos emerges order, a clean cut
                          removing earth's excrescences:
My pavilion soars and I float with the clouds.

Distant peaks in neat array converge on us;
The winding river clasps its green banks in farewell.
The evening glows as the sun sinks beneath us;
The birds return to their perch under our gaze.

The lake overbrims with the pink of lotus flowers;
The bamboos—a host of righteous men—
                       parade in our presence.
My spirit is eased, all shackles now thrown off,
My heart content, secret tears of grief forgotten.

Rejected by my prince, long wasting away in sorrow,
Today I break afresh into laughter.
For men of a like mind need not abide together,[2]
But separation intensifies their mutual concern.

To the north, I look out for loved ones I am divided from,
And to the south, friends scattered among
                     barbarous tribesmen.
I will dismiss such thoughts nor speak of them again—
Let this moment be for me all time and all the world!

[1] c. 43, pp. 714–15. Fa-hua Temple, situated on a mountain peak to the east of Lingling, is the subject of an earlier poem by Liu; see p. 106.
[2] 'Men of a like mind', etc.: another echo of Hsieh Ling-yün, though this may not be obvious from the poems in the Chapter on Hsieh, *supra*.

West Pavilion by Fa-hua Temple[1]
(809)

Fa-hua Temple is situated in the prefecture of Yung-chou, of which it marks the highest point. There the monk Chüeh-chao ['Perceptive Illumination'] has his cell, by the porch of the western wing of the temple. The porch is shaded by thousands of tall and stately bamboos, beyond which is a steep precipice. The precipice was, however, hidden and the view blocked by shrubs and untidy bamboos and a dense undergrowth. Feeling certain that the removal of this tangled mass would reveal an interesting prospect, I consulted Chüeh-chao, who said: 'There is a large lotus pond below. The river Hsiang stretches out before one, and the hills are in the distance. If you do clear away the thicket, you will see far afield.'

Thereupon I ordered the servants to take knives and axes and cut down the shrubs and straggly bamboos, which soon lay in heaps underfoot. A myriad objects now presented themselves. What an expanse! How much vaster now the world! The sky lifted; the earth grew wider. Cliffs and hills rose to new eminence; river and lake increased in extent. In my banishment I was Marshal Extraordinary of the prefecture, a post with no regular duties but ample leisure. And realising that so wonderful a scene had to be preserved for future generations without being allowed to fall again into neglect, I erected with part of my salary a pavilion on the site, its dimensions being twenty feet square and the height also twenty feet.

Some have expressed surprise that Chüeh-chao, who lived there, had not earlier attended to such a task. I explain it thus: the monks of old, without rising from their posture of meditation, were able to discern the reality behind form and emptiness, and be at one with the beginning and end of things. Their 'illumination' reached beyond stillness; their 'perception' transcended existence. This being so, what formerly obscured the view was to the monk no real obstacle, nor the present prospect a truly widened horizon. He who styles him-

[1] c. 28, pp. 463–4.

self 'Perceptive Illumination' follows other paths than we, who in our anxiety to break down barriers merely hem ourselves in. It being then suggested that I should record the event, I do so upon this stone.

Preface to the Poems written at a gathering of friends in West Pavilion[1]
(810)

Being in Yung-chou in my state of banishment, I found that Fa-hua Temple overlooked on its west side a lake and hills, and, moreover, the mighty current of the Hsiang river, which flows through mountain gorges. Though situated at a considerable height, the temple was not inaccessible, and from it the view reached out to a great distance. I, therefore, had some trees felled and a pavilion built there, so as to be able to watch the scenery in wind and rain, and study the elemental forces, and be uplifted to the highest stratum of the all-embracing atmosphere.

In the following year—the censor Yüan K'e-chi having earlier been banished and come this way, followed not long afterwards by my younger literary friends, nearly all of whom were by then assembled in Yung-chou—eight of us met in the pavilion one evening. After a sumptuous repast with wine, the censor expressed a wish to have the occasion commemorated, and asked the rest of us to write poems, to which I was to contribute the Preface.

When, as recorded in the Tso Commentary,[2] Chao Meng visited the State of Cheng, he requested the seven courtiers of Cheng each to sing one of the Odes, his intention was to ascertain the state of mind of those who inhabited Cheng. It may thus be deduced that Censor Yüan was an admirer of Chao Meng. The disciple Tzu-hsia wrote the Preface to the Book of Poetry[3] in order that later generations might under-

---

[1] c. 24, pp. 409–10.
[2] Legge, *The Chinese Classics*, Vol. v, *The Ch'un Ts'ew with the Tso Chuen*, Book ix, Duke Seang, Year xxvii, pp. 533–4.
[3] For the Preface to the Book of Poetry, see 'The Great Preface' in Volume iii of this series.

stand the Songs of the various States as well as the Odes of the
Kingdom. It may, therefore, be thought that I was a follower
of Tzu-hsia. Should these our compositions indeed survive
the ravages of time, then perhaps the comparison might come
to seem not so utterly far-fetched.

[Liu's poem[1] written on that occasion has been preserved. It
reads:]

At sunset, in the temple pavilion,
We quaff this quintessential drink.

Veiled by the mist, the lake steals up to our threshold;
Revelling in the moonlight, flowers print their
                                                    shadows on the window.
Let me drink nor fear intoxication,
Rejoicing in the youthful fellowship.

The Three Pavilions of Lingling[2]

That a county should have ornamental buildings with ex-
tensive views is a proposition often dismissed as irrelevant to
government and local affairs, but this is quite wrong. For if
the spirit is vexed, the process of thought will be disturbed;
and if one's sight is obstructed, one's outlook will be con-
fined. He who would govern must be able to repair for rest
and refreshment to familiar haunts in the shapes of towers and
elevated structures so as to restore his mind to tranquillity and
equanimity with a sufficient reserve of strength. Only then
will reason prevail and deeds be accomplished.

To the east of the county town of Lingling, a fountain welled
out of the rocks at the foot of a hill, wetting the ground and
transforming a small surrounding area into a patch of muddy
slime. The farm animals would crowd round it to drink of the
spring water, and a fence had to be set up to hide the eyesore.
This fence was allowed to remain there under a succession of

---

[1] c. 43, p. 726.
[2] c. 27, pp. 457–8. Lingling, the county town, was also the seat of the
prefecture of Yung-chou.

over a score of magistrates, not one of whom inquired why it was there. Then came Magistrate Hsüeh Ts'un-i of Ho-tung (i.e., Shansi Province), who had made his reputation as an able officer in the Ching and Ch'u regions (i.e., Hupeh and Hunan Provinces) and, on the recommendation of the Provincial Governor, had been seconded as Magistrate of Hsiang-yüan, also of the Prefecture of Yung-chou. Lingling was at the time suffering from bad government and multifarious taxation, and the people complained to the Prefect, who then had Magistrate Hsüeh transferred to the county to redress the grievances. Thereupon, those previously in flight or in hiding returned to their homes; the anxious and afflicted burst into song and laughter; rents in arrears were paid and services untendered supplied within the month; those who had concealed their crimes and past misdeeds made a clean breast of their offences. The people, from whom only an equitable share of the taxes was now exacted, paid it with alacrity and returned with relief along the highways, greeting and congratulating one another at the entrance to their villages. Their gates were no longer invaded by petty officials who had to be feasted; their ears were unmolested by the sound of drums summoning them to statute labour. Their farm produce—chickens and pork and crisp rice-cake and home-brewed wine—they were able to keep for themselves and share with their clansmen. The county won the praise of the Prefect, and neighbouring counties sought to emulate its achievement.

In his state of calm detachment and self-possession, the Magistrate had hitherto, on account of the press of affairs, not troubled to cultivate the enjoyment of landscape, birds and fish. At this point, he had the fence removed, drove off the animals, dredged the slime, and cleaned up the hill-side. Thousands of stones were piled up into a vast rockery, and a pond was made under the fountain. Trees and ornamental plants were laid out on the slopes along the pond, as well as near the hill-top, their leafy branches rustling mournfully in the cool breezes. Thin mists curled among the green vegetation, which thrived without further cultivation. Fish disported themselves in the spacious pond; passing birds stayed to nest in the seclusion of the trees and rocks; and thus the voluntary inhabitants of aviary and piscina multiplied. Furthermore, the trees felled drifted down the river to the very gate of the county administration, where they served as posts in a mud wall being erected to the side of the county buildings. Thus with no extra effort, much benefit accrued to the public works. It was then that the three pavilions were built. These were sited at different levels, enjoying varying degrees of light and shade. The highest was situated on the peak; the lowest immediately overlooked the pond. Facilities were now to be had for a change of clothing, for cooked meals, for social gatherings and banqueting, and for the rest of travellers.

Thus the building of towers and pavilions for recreation began in this county with Magistrate Hsüeh. In the Tso Commentary,[1] the resourceful P'i Ch'en of the State of Cheng invariably repaired to the country to plan his successful stratagems. And the disciple Fu Pu-ch'i, under whose magistracy the district of Shan-fu prospered, was generally to be seen playing on his guitar. For if one's thoughts are unsettled and one's outlook confined, one will find no room for fresh ideas, for which reason I maintain that ornamental buildings with extensive views do form part of government and local affairs. And one might infer that this was Magistrate Hsüeh's aim. To be sure, the attitude could lead to abuse, with sport displacing government and careless neglect encroaching on the orderly dispatch of business. But if all his successors should have the same aim as Magistrate Hsüeh, then the blessings he has conferred on the people of the county would be much prolonged.[2] I commend the excellent start he has made and wish to see his course of action continued, and have therefore written this account on stone. Magistrate Hsüeh now declaring with a bow that his aim was indeed as stated above, I order the words to be carved.

---

[1] Legge, *The Chinese Classics*, Vol. v, *The Ch'un Ts'ew with the Tso Chuen*, Book ix, Duke Seang, Year xxxi, p. 565.
[2] Liu is equally complimentary in his farewell address to Hsüeh (c. 23, pp. 391–2) at the end of Hsüeh's term of office, which lasted two years. It may be of interest to note that, like Liu's family, Hsüeh was from Shansi.

The Pavilion on Ma-t'ui Mountain
in Yung-ning[1] (Nanning)
(811)

It was in the tenth month, early in winter, that a new pavilion was built on the southern side of Ma-t'ui Mountain, full advantage being taken in its siting and structure of the shelter provided by a recession in the declivity. Thus there was no need for such ornaments as carved beams and capitals; no trees were felled for its rafters; no thatch was prepared for its roof; no walls were erected; the white clouds served as fence, the green hills as screen. Its construction was a shining example of thrift as prescribed by the ancients.

Ma-t'ui Mountain is the chief link in a chain of hills stretching across scores of li. They are hills rising sheer from the tangled vegetation on the ground precipitately into the region of the clouds. The last of the hills penetrates into uninhabited country, and the torrents of the first disembogue into the great stream [i.e., the Left River or River Yü, a tributary of the Sikiang]. The hills converge on Ma-t'ui Mountain as in homage, the contrasting shades of grass and leaf being heightened by the fantastic shapes of the hills themselves into such patterns as are only seen on woven fabrics and embroidery. For heaven has chosen to endow this border region with extraordinary beauty. Since, however, the prefecture adjoins the wild wastes and its customs are not unmixed with those of the tribesmen, no royal progress has graced its hill-sides and the mountain-climber with his Hsieh Ling-yün boots[2] has never set foot in it. And this is lamented by all who have had the opportunity of exploring its cliffs and paths.

The year was hsin-mao [811], and my cousin had been sent out to be Prefect. His perfect virtue engendered trust, and trust engendered harmony among the people, and harmony among the people reduced litigation and crime, so that the Prefect had much leisure. Thus on one occasion he visited

[1] c. 27, pp. 453–4. The prefecture, whose name in romanisation was also Yung-chou, was hundreds of kilometres south of our poet's Yung-chou; it is therefore referred to by its later name Yung-ning (today, Nanning in Kwangsi Province).
[2] See Chapter on Hsieh Ling-yün, supra.

Ma-t'ui Mountain and lingered to admire the scenery. And it
was then that he decided to build the pavilion—

'They painted the ceiling, they painted the walls,
And lo! the house was ready.'

For the carpenters, it was but a morning's work. And when it
was fine and the winds were still, and the mists lifted to reveal
the clouds arrayed in all their glory, he would change into a
deerskin jacket and a hermit's cap, and walk up to the
mountain top with half a dozen hatted gentlemen, being his
brothers, friends and students. There, with his hand on the
guitar and his eyes following the floating clouds, he would
imbibe the exhilarating mountain air, while all creation was
spread out before him, to be scanned like his own palm.

For beauty exists not for itself, but for the beholder, who
enhances it. Without Wang Hsi-chih, Lan-t'ing Pavilion,[1] for
all its clear streams and tall, stately bamboos, would have lain
buried and forgotten in the hills of Kuei-chi. As for this
pavilion, situated on a remote barbarous mountain and
seldom visited by those in search of delightful scenery, with-
out some record of the purpose for which it was built, it would
certainly sink into oblivion, to the lasting regret of the woods
and torrents. And so I have written this account of it.

Ten Thousand Rocks Pavilion[2]
(815)

The Deputy Principal Censor, Baron Ts'ui of Ch'ing-ho [i.e.,
Hopei Province] having come to Yung-chou as Prefect, as-
cended the northern ramparts of the town wall on a day when
he was free, and noticed strangely shaped rocks jutting out
from a tall heap of tangled vegetation. Realising that they
indicated the presence of some unusually picturesque sight
concealed by the undergrowth, he went on a walk from the
West Gate in search of the mound. To enable him to penetrate
the jungle, some bamboos had to be cut down, after which he

[1] For Wang Hsi-chih and Lan-t'ing Pavilion, see 'General Introduc-
tion'.
[2] c. 27, pp. 455–7.

was able to sidle along. He found countless rocks straddling a small ravine and stream, like flocks of clouds driven by the wind or chess pieces locked in odd formations on a two-hundred-and-fifty-six-squared board.[1] Their shapes, too, were striking: some crouching nervously like a tiger about to pounce, others tensely poised on a tapering base like an excited crane. They seemed so alive that if one poked into a hole one half expected to be greeted by a snout or snarling teeth, and if one brushed against their lower surfaces one feared to meet a rump or hoof. They appeared to be ring upon ring of startled beasts ready to attack or bite.

The Prefect then set about clearing the hillock and ravine, removing the thorns and tangled growth, which he burnt, and bringing into prominence a few fine trees previously obscured by the brushwood. A drain was dug to channel the waters of hidden streams into a newly made pond. In place of the jungle, there was now a wide open space with a clear stretch of water. It was as if the creator himself with his miraculous powers had fashioned order out of chaos.[2] And the Prefect then built a pavilion on the slope, so situated as to afford a breathless view of a narrow cleft in the rock a little to its west: looking down the cleft, one gained the impression of green precipices descending into some pool of unfathomable depth; on one's looking up, the same precipices seemed to rise to unending height, their lines almost meeting at the top.

On the day after the completion of the pavilion, a motley crowd of elders from the county and the prefecture arrived to address the Prefect, saying, 'We were born in this prefecture and tilled our fields in these wilds. Our eyebrows have turned grey and our teeth have fallen out, but never in our lives did we know of the existence of these stones. We verily believe that they fell down from the sky or sprouted out of the earth

[1] Unlike the modern chess ('go') board, which has 324 squares, the T'ang chessboard had only 256.
[2] A parallel passage from 'The Hill of the Rock Hall' (c. 29, p. 476) (812), another Yung-chou essay, reads: 'I have long debated with myself the question of the existence of a creator, and the sight of this [hill with its trees so laid out among the rocks as to suggest a mind at work] confirms my opinion that a creator exists, which makes me wonder why such a pride of creation was not placed in the central provinces but in the regions of the barbarians'.

as a sign of divine approval of your virtue.' And after con-
gratulating the Prefect, they entreated that he would name
the pavilion. The Prefect replied: 'I cannot tell the exact
number of the stones here. Since they are legion, I will name
this pavilion "Ten Thousand Rocks Pavilion".' The elders
then said, 'And a most appropriate name you have conferred
on it, for "Ten Thousand Rocks" not only describes its sur-
rounding objects, but also its illustrious patron! You, our
Prefect, have held for six terms a "Two Thousand Picul-
stone"[1] post, and are thus equivalent to, nay exceed, ten
thousand stones. However, men of discernment have often
regretted that your meritorious achievements have not been
more widely commemorated:

> Let us sing your praises on this occasion
> And may the gods hear these our words!
> The three pillars of state in the Han
> Were jointly known as 'Ministers of Ten Thousand
>   Picul-stone':[2]
> The virtue of our Prefect
> Is worthy of even such an honourable designation,
> Or that of officials of the highest distinction,
> Known as 'Lords of Ten Thousand Picul-stone'![3]
> For the sagacity of our Prefect
> Was fostered even in the nursery;
> His ways are in accord with ancient practice,
> And heaven has seen fit to reward him.
> A final wish from us uncouth rustics —
> May your life, too, last in years ten thousand!'

[1] Picul-stone: the usual word is picul, a grain measure of the weight
133⅓ lbs. In the original, the word *shih* means, however, stone or rock
as well as a grain measure; the pun is somewhat diluted in the render-
ing—'picul-stone'. In the Han dynasty, the approximate amount of
rice which an official received as his annual stipend was an indication
of his rank. Prefects were of the rank known as 'Two Thousand Picul-
stone'.
[2] In the Han, the combined stipends of the three Chief Ministers
exceeded ten thousand picul-stone, and they were jointly referred to
as 'Ministers of Ten Thousand Picul-stone'.
[3] Five members of the same family each holding a 'Two Thousand
Picul-stone' post in the Han were referred to as 'Lords of Ten
Thousand Picul-stone'.

I, Liu Tsung-yüan, having previously taken note of this event in a report to the Secretary of State, now venture to make a special record of it as a supplement to the traditions of Lingling on this fifth day of the first month in the tenth year of the *Yüan-ho* reign.[1]

Eastern Mound by Lung-hsing Temple[2]

Those in quest of interesting scenery take delight chiefly in two types of view: the expanse and spaciousness of the open view, and the immediate impact and hidden mysteries of the confined view. Where the ground rises steeply over potential obstructions or breaks through thick vegetation to give an impression of vast space and distance, it is suited to the open view. Where a hillock or mound intrudes or shrubs and undergrowth lie in concealment to offer unexpected scenes at every turn, the spot is more suited to the confined view. Where an open view presents itself, one may enhance its attraction by building raised terraces and projecting pavilions, to enable the rambler to follow the revolving motions of the sun and the stars or to watch a storm in progress; and it would be idle to complain that the view is too sweeping. Where a confined view presents itself, one may also enhance its attraction by planting trees with rich foliage or piling up rocks, to suggest the effect of a grotto or recess or arbour or clearing; and it would likewise be idle to complain that the view is too restricted.

That which I call Eastern Mound offers the confined view. To begin with, it was waste land outside the temple grounds. When I bought it, I joined it to the temple, to whose north-eastern glade[3] it formed an extension. Without disturbing its natural contours, which included hollows and cavities, swamps and islets, I had a thick screen of bamboos planted, and a bridge with many bends built across the swamps. And I also

---

[1] The essay would seem to be the last one written by Liu Tsung-yüan in Yung-chou. In the same month of that year (815), he was recalled to the capital, which he reached in the second month.

[2] c. 28, pp. 462–3.

[3] The glade situated to the north-east of Lung-hsing Temple is the subject of another essay (c. 28, pp. 461–2) by Liu.

had nearly three hundred trees planted, including cinnamon, juniper, pine, fir, catalpa and cedar. I then had ornamental plants and rocks laid out in criss-cross patterns all over the mound. The ground was now a carpet of green grass, and the trees provided shade and seclusion; and in this labyrinth wanderers often found that they no longer knew the route by which they had entered. The air was balmy without being oppressive, for there would usually be a cool breeze. A water pavilion and a hut further added to the interest of this example of the confined view.

And yet visitors have been heard to remark on its narrow and restricted views as a shortcoming. Shortcoming indeed! Lung-hsing, so prominently situated, is, to be sure, a temple of which the district may well feel proud. From its towers one may salute the 'Old Man' star;[1] a re-sited main gate has opened up the prospect of the river Hsiang and its valley. In short, a pre-eminent example of the open view. But to accord the same treatment to this little mound and denude it by removing its trees and vegetation would cause it to lose its natural advantages. And this would be to reduce what I maintain to be the two types of view to a single one. For indeed—

Eastern Mound is a secluded place,
> Where the weary traveller may rest his feet;
Eastern Mound is dark and mysterious,
> Yet there is much to delight the eye;
The foot of Eastern Mound
> Provides a retreat from the muggy heat;
At the top of Eastern Mound
> Joyfully the people congregate;
I will admit it, the view is confined—
> Will no one wander there with me?

Being without the awe-inspiring virtues of Duke Shao,[2] whose people kept his memory green after his death by jealously guarding his favourite tree, I do greatly fear the descent of shears and axes upon this my mound. And so I address this appeal to gentlemen of a future age who may hold opinions different from mine in regard to landscape views.

[1] The 'Old Man' star: Canopus.
[2] Duke Shao, founder of the ruling house of Yen in the Chou dynasty.